Parrot Tricks

Parrot Tricks

Teaching Parrots with Positive Reinforcement

Tani Robar and Diane Grindol

Library of Congress Cataloging-in-Publication Data:
Robar, Tani.
Parrot tricks / Tani Robar and Diane Grindol.
    p. cm.
    Includes index.
    ISBN-13: 978-0-7645-8461-9 (alk. paper)
    ISBN-10: 0-7645-8461-8 (alk. paper)
    1. Parrots—Training. I. Grindol, Diane. II. Title.
    SF473.P3R55 2006
    636.6'86535—dc22   2005024915

Printed in the United States of America

10 9 8 7 6 5 4 3 2 1

Book design by Marie Kristine Parial-Leonardo
Cover design by Michael Rutkowski
Book production by Wiley Publishing, Inc. Composition Services

Contents

Foreword

Over my thirty years of working with companion parrots, it has become very clear that these intelligent birds thrive on what I call "instructional interaction." One of the greatest advantages of teaching tricks or positive behaviors to a companion parrot is the ability to use them to redirect negative behaviors. My 16-year-old Caique, Spikey LeBec, can be a real terror at times, even with me. If he is so stubborn and/or wound-up that he is difficult for me to handle, I have him do a somersault in my hand and tell him what a good boy he is. He is quickly distracted from his antsy aggression and gives me his attention almost immediately. All of my parrots have at least one or two trained behaviors that they do for praise and attention. These include somersaults, raising a foot to "gimme four," whistling duets, hopping across a table, rolling over on their backs, or spreading their wings to the cue, "Eagle Boy."

They are simple tricks, and we do not take ourselves too seriously about them because they are totally for our enjoyment and not to impress anyone. Years ago when I used to do a monthly parrot care seminar at a local humane society, I had trained Spike to put a wiffle ball through a miniature basketball hoop. He was very good at it. Unfortunately the ball rolled off the table one too many times. Each time a very helpful person from the audience would reach down and pick up the ball and give it to Spike. Of course the audience laughed because they thought it was very funny when he rolled the ball off of the table and then looked at the audience with his imploring body language. It only took a few times for him to realize it was a lot more fun to get someone to pick up the ball for him than it was for him to put it in the hoop. So much for Spikey being the star attraction in a parrot show!

Tricks are simply positive behaviors that have been trained by giving the parrot a consistent positive reward through patterning. Why does it work so well with our companion parrots? Because it provides them with one extremely important factor that they need to be happy in our lives—focused attention from the people in their lives. When many people think of giving their parrots attention, they think of cuddling and physical affection. A certain amount of this is fine, but the people who realize that instructional interaction is the most positive way to relate to an intelligent parrot are the ones who have the most successful relationships with their birds.

I have seen lots of parrots doing tricks over the years, but the most memorable ones are not the ones that are most technically accomplished, but those where the love and respect in the relationship shine through, and it is obvious that both the people and the parrots are having fun. This is why I enjoy Tani Robar and her performing parrots. Like my Caique, Spike, sometimes her Caique, Cassie, seems to get distracted and loves the attention of the audience so much that she doesn't do all of her tricks exactly on cue. Instead of climbing a ladder, she hops away from it. But it is all in good fun, and Tani exhibits great patience in redirecting Cassie to the task at hand. Laughter from the audience clearly proves that they prefer this type of friendly interaction rather than that of a robotlike automaton performing rote tricks.

—Sally Blanchard
Editor, *Companion Parrot Quarterly*

Acknowledgments

Many of the photos in this book are from the authors' personal collections. We would like to thank the following photographers who graciously supplied other photos for this book:

Barbara Kinney, Photography
John Clisold, The Photo Pro
Judy Murphy
Keith Robar
Doris Wilmoth

We also would like to thank David Marak of Kansas City, Missouri, for his contributions to the drawings of the props in chapter 13. The drawings don't begin to showcase his talent as an artist, but as always, he was a willing and helpful contributor to this book.

Introduction

If you love birds, have an ordinary amount of patience, and are willing to work with your bird several times a week, you can train your own bird as well as an expert could—perhaps better, as no one else knows your bird as well as you do. Training a bird has too often been presented as a long, drawn-out process involving much study, special "tricks," and even negative feelings toward the bird.

Psychologists have provided us with all sorts of insights to refine and speed up the training process and the trainee's level of performance. But, in this book, you'll get very little theory. Instead you'll find proven, step-by-step instructions to train your bird to do all kinds of tricks. You're going to get a clearer understanding of the process of training and learn how to better communicate with your pet.

Throughout this book I will be sharing my personal experiences gained training various companion parrots. The tricks in this book are all behaviors I have personally taught. My co-author, Diane Grindol, has lent her editing, writing, and photography skills to this project.

Please be sure to notice that I recommend no physical punishment for your bird. It is not necessary, and it is not deserved. When you see a well-trained bird obeying every command of his master, notice particularly the eagerness the bird shows for his handler's commands. If he is not happily anticipating each new command, he has not been trained correctly. Birds love to do tricks; they don't judge tricks as silly or useless; they don't even look for a reason for doing a trick; they just like what they're doing. Contrast this behavior with that of some birds who have never been trained. Such poor animals go through life in confusion, never knowing for sure what is expected of them—praised one moment for one thing, punished the next for doing the same, or what seems to them to be the same, act. These unfortunate birds, with sympathetic training, would learn to mind cheerfully and would live much happier lives as would their owners and anyone coming in contact with these birds. Teaching tricks has tamed many a bird, increased their bonds with their humans, and enriched the lives of both.

In the following pages I have given specific directions for training many routines. The greatest value of training for your bird does not lie, however, in teaching him these relatively few accomplishments, important though they are. It is in the fact that, by this training, you condition him to obey you in every way, without question. You and your bird will become very close to each other, will understand each other, and will come to love and respect each other as neither would without this firm basis of master and willing subject.

And, yes, I would love to have you experience performing for appreciative audiences with a bird who is a ham. I would love you to be the next contestant on *Pet Star*. But if you never do a trick outside your living room, or if you never get beyond the *step up* and the *come* commands, you can still love and appreciate your bird. Don't forget the reasons you wanted a pet bird. Trick training was probably not your first priority in choosing a companion parrot. You wanted a beautiful bird; you wanted a companion; and you have him. If your bird does not like performing, he probably still likes showers with you and the friendly repartee between you and him as you bustle about your home. Be aware of how life is for you and your bird and appreciate what you have.

As an involved parrot owner working on training, chances are good that you'll keep your companion parrot in your home. Thank you for taking the time to work with your bird and for offering him an interesting, stable home life. You're in for an exciting time. What can you expect of life with a bird? Fun and games, creativity and stimulation, and a pet who challenges your intellect. You probably will become curious about other birds, their wild counterparts, and their interesting behavior. You'll buy vegetables and fruits you never would have before, in order to feed your bird a variety of food. You'll buy toys to entertain your bird and send off mail orders for toys that you can't find locally. You'll carry a picture of your bird in your wallet. Who needs TV with a bird in the house? Opening the cage and watching a bird eat and play is great entertainment. And as your bird settles into your family, you probably will wonder how you ever got along without him in your life.

In using this book, do read chapters 2 ("Preparations for Training"), 3 ("Training Basics"), and 4 ("Necessary Obedience Skills [Husbandry Behaviors]") before starting to train tricks. I have put all the background material in them to make you a good trainer. Further, just for the ease in writing the book and so you don't get confused, I will be referring to your parrots during all the training chapters as "he" and to the people doing the training as "she." The exceptions will be when I am talking about my own birds and experiences with them. My birds are all females, so when I am talking about them I will be referring to them as "she." There are probably many ways to teach some of these tricks; there is no one "right" way. The methods I have described are all ones I have used successfully in teaching various parrots tricks and so recommend them.

Be patient, gentle, and understanding. Don't try to hurry your bird along too fast. You're going to have a lot of fun working together, and you'll both be proud of each other and yourselves when the job is done.

—Tani Robar

Chapter *1*

The Advantages of Trick Training Your Parrot

When you work with a companion bird in order to teach him *tricks* or *behaviors,* the bond and communication between the two of you increases dramatically. Trick training involves interaction with your bird. This interaction is structured and leads to results that are exciting for both of you. Your bird is excited about both learning from you and communicating with you. He lives in a world with beings who do not speak his language. He has behaviors that enhance life in his native habitat, for which he and his body and instincts are designed. When your parrot can understand some of what you ask of him, there is progress made in communication and mutual respect. As soon as your parrot has learned that he can do what you ask and get something he values (a treat or a head scratch) in return, he will want to learn more. Learning becomes easier for him, and that makes teaching easier for you. You will undoubtedly learn much from your bird, too.

BENEFITS TO YOU

A bird must be taught with patience, love, and nurturing. No punishment should be involved. You will be teaching your bird behaviors in small steps. You can't expect a bird to see a trick and then execute it perfectly. You will be breaking a trick down to shorter behaviors. This is an exercise in patience and planning. Over time, these behaviors will lead to the performance of cute acts or more complicated tricks. The more behaviors your parrot learns, the more he is likely to learn, and the better communication you will have with your parrot.

It is fulfilling for you to watch your bird make progress. Progress leads to pride in your bird so that you spend more time working with him and even start taking him with you to show off his tricks to others. You look forward to training sessions.

4

At times your parrot will be trying to learn a behavior but just not catching on. Even that experience can benefit you. When one method of training is not working, you will need to think of other ways to train that behavior. This spurs your creative juices.

Many aspects of trick training offer creative outlets for owners. You are being creative when you choose a trick to train and when you interact with your parrot in order to communicate. It can be exciting (and a bit taxing) to develop the cross-species communication needed to train tricks to a companion bird. Putting tricks together into an act is creative. Developing a monologue or a story line to go with your tricks is also a creative exercise. Even finding places to perform with your bird can be creative.

Many tricks in this book are performed with simple props. Some of these props require some creative woodworking on your part or finding a person who can build props in a size appropriate for your bird. Other props are found objects, so you'll be stretching your creative muscles in looking at objects and imagining how your bird could interact with them and how you could work them into a story line.

BENEFITS TO YOUR BIRD

Your companion bird is an intelligent and social animal. Keeping birds as we do in small spaces (compared to, say, a rain forest or savannah) with a limited number of things to do is not very natural. It's a testimony to the adaptability of parrots that they get along as well as they do in human environments. Parrots move into our homes and readily learn our language, eat cut-up food from cups, and chew on the cabinetry and molding in our homes instead of tree branches found in their native habitat. Our parrots forage on carpeting, nest in cabinets, and bond with flock mates of different species. They call to the microwave instead of fellow parrots and do their best to spread vegetable matter on the forest floor to enrich the poor soil at the base of their cages.

For your bird, it is a good use of his natural intelligence and inquisitive nature to learn tricks. There are new things to figure out, just as he would be figuring out weather conditions, foraging areas, and places to roost in the wild. You will find that your bird, no matter what his size, has an enormous capacity to learn and retain many kinds of tricks. Exposure to new tricks and behaviors during his lifetime lets him use his native intelligence.

Not only does your bird enjoy exercising his brain when learning tricks, but learning tricks offers him needed attention and socialization. Trick training lessons are time spent out of his cage and engaged with one of his favorite people—you. You're willing to give him this attention now and in the future, as you both progress in your trick-training skills. You'll be offering your parrot a much more interesting life!

SOCIALIZATION

One of the things our companion parrots need and appreciate most from us is simply *more* of us. Regular training lessons are one way to spend quality time with your companion parrot. Success in training inspires more time spent training, which is fine with your parrot and makes him even happier.

If you have a baby bird, he is at a stage in which he would be learning many things from his parent birds and other flock members. He would be learning flock calls, how to identify dangers, how to spend his time, and how to maintain his feathers and vigor. He would learn how to fly, how to identify edible vegetation, and how to choose a roost spot at night. A baby bird learns to bathe, preen, and interact with other birds in his early months and years of life. When you acquire a companion bird, you and your family members become his flock, and he expects to learn from you. Go ahead and teach him some things!

MAKING LIFE EASIER

Life is better when you live with a trained bird. Your bird probably thinks so, too. In this case, I'm not talking about cute tricks, but rather day-to-day habits. You can *obedience train* your companion bird to some extent. Your bird is anxious to learn and willing to communicate with you. You make it worth his time to comply with you. You both will have less stressful lives if he knows how to go to bed quietly, get in a carrier, offer a claw for nail clipping, or accept a ride back to his cage without a fuss when you head off to work.

It's become common to teach a bird to step onto your hand or a stick on command. I discuss this in several places in this book, as it's essential training for a parrot. In addition, your parrot should learn other words and behaviors. You aren't going to show these behaviors off, necessarily, but you will enjoy the rewards of training every day. Your bird is a quick study. You won't have to spend much time teaching him the simple behaviors that make a big difference in your life—and in the life of your parrot.

Your bird can learn to stay put on a play gym, with persistent reminders about the rules. He can learn to potty in designated places, fly to you on command, and climb a ladder back to his cage so that he is not wandering around underfoot. The rewards of obedience training your bird are tremendous. You'll probably astound your friends. You might not even notice how you and your bird interact after a while. Life will be easier, freeing you up to think about the possibility of teaching your bird some tricks!

A NEW EXPERIENCE FOR YOU

If you love pets and have had experience with dogs and cats in the past, you'll notice that a bird is different. Of course, birds have feathers, and dogs and cats do not! But there is a basic difference between predators like dogs and cats and prey animals like parrots. Birds are wary of new things and experiences because that very awareness could save their lives in the wild. Like people, dogs and cats have eyes in the front of their head, whereas birds have eyes on the side of their head to increase their chances of spotting a predator. We can't imagine how they see with eyes on opposite sides of their head and peripheral vision that includes areas in front of and behind them. You'll notice that when your bird is intent on something, he will train one eye on it and stare at it that way.

Birds also see colors, unlike our dog companions who see the world in shades of gray. We supply birds with colorful toys for that reason. Birds have highly developed senses of sight and hearing, whereas dogs and cats have exceptional smell and taste. You get to know a new dog by giving him your hand to smell. A parrot is watching your actions, and you'll make friends best by offering food, using slow careful movements, and speaking in a soft voice—actions that appeal to a parrot's keen vision, awareness of body language, and sharp hearing. Parrots have about one tenth the number of taste buds as a person; eating a hot pepper for breakfast is enjoyable for a bird, but he won't spend a lot of time smelling and tasting food to determine its desirability. A bird will look at the color of food, enjoy its texture, and use his beak to test its temperature.

Dogs and cats have been humankind's companion animals for thousands of generations. They have been domesticated by humans, and many breeds of each species have been developed for specific tasks that aid people, like herding sheep, retrieving fowl after a hunt, and just sitting on laps to be adored. Some of our parrots, or at least our parrot's parents and grandparents, were flying free in their native environment just a few years ago. There are more than 300 species of parrots, each adapted to a different native environment and with different needs. They are still mostly identical to wild-type parrots. Contrast that with the one species dog with many man-made breeds that don't exist in the wild, and the one species cat that also has many man-made breeds that we keep as pets. Most parrots cannot be considered domesticated. They are still wild animals, the companion bird equivalent of keeping a wolf or an ocelot instead of a dog or a cat as a pet. Many of our current parrot pets did come from the wild, or their parents or grandparents did. Even the "domesticated" species of birds like Cockatiels and Budgies have been kept in captivity for fewer than 200 years. Dogs have been domesticated for 15,000 years, and there have been changes over that time, with breeds developed to meet the needs of humans. The parrot species we keep do still exist in the wild and were not developed by humans to meet their needs. We are changing some species of birds, such as the colors of Cockatiels, Lovebirds, Quaker Parakeets, and Indian Ring-necked Parakeets. And we've changed not only the color but the form of Budgies and Zebra Finches. But these changes involve mutations and do not have anything to do with changing their usefulness to us.

Dogs have been bred to serve man and faithfully look to us for guidance and approval. Cats are more independent but have lived in proximity to people for a long time, catching vermin and warming laps. The importance of this in day-to-day life with our wild companion parrots is that they do not seek to please us. Parrots are very self-centered and self-serving pets. Your job in seeking to win their trust and in shaping their behavior is to find a way to do so that gives a bird what he wants. Parrots are motivated by food and interaction. By having regular training lessons with your pet parrot, you are providing him with both of his favorite things: interaction and food. It's a win-win situation!

BIRD AMBASSADORSHIP: GETTING OUT WITH YOUR PARROT

Take your parrot with you to visit friends, neighbors, and relatives. It is good for your parrot's confidence to learn how to behave in other situations and in homes other than yours. Getting out with your parrot will expose him to people of different sizes and colors. In other homes he'll see walls that are colored differently and people who have facial hair, wear hats, or have/don't have hair on their heads. Over time, your bird will build confidence and poise around others through these trips and exposure to different situations.

Your bird will probably be delighted to do what you want in response to a verbal or a visual cue. After a bird discovers how to learn, he really blossoms. Every time you take your bird out there is a side benefit. Although *you* know how engrossing and entertaining your companion bird can be, many people in our society have not been exposed to birds as pets since their grandmother had a canary or since their childhood budgie died. Good bird care is not common knowledge in our society. You will probably spark some interest by being in public with your companion bird. You might find yourself talking to people about what birds eat, how they live in a home, and what it's like to live with a bird. Many people don't know that companion birds need regular baths, that they can be killed by overheated nonstick cookware, or that they can share our meals with us.

As an enthusiastic bird owner, you become a public ambassador for bird ownership. Be truthful and tell the whole story! Birds do bite, scream, throw food around, and tear up toys. They require time and energy and a certain amount of money. But they also return to us affection and companionship. Their antics make us laugh. The love and enthusiasm for your bird shining in your eyes will speak volumes.

KEEP YOUR EXPECTATIONS IN CHECK

Many companion birds end up in rescue and parrot adoption centers through no fault of their own. These birds did not meet the expectations of their human

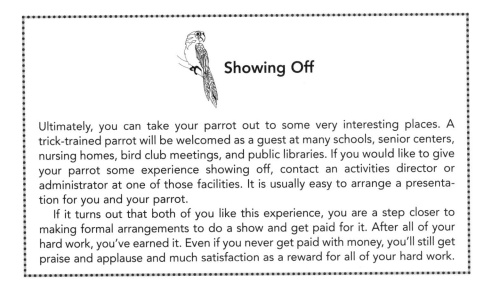

Showing Off

Ultimately, you can take your parrot out to some very interesting places. A trick-trained parrot will be welcomed as a guest at many schools, senior centers, nursing homes, bird club meetings, and public libraries. If you would like to give your parrot some experience showing off, contact an activities director or administrator at one of those facilities. It is usually easy to arrange a presentation for you and your parrot.

If it turns out that both of you like this experience, you are a step closer to making formal arrangements to do a show and get paid for it. After all of your hard work, you've earned it. Even if you never get paid with money, you'll still get praise and applause and much satisfaction as a reward for all of your hard work.

companions. Their owners probably wanted quiet sweet birds; they wanted birds like the neighbor's entertaining and well-loved bird, or they wanted birds who didn't scream or didn't throw food around. They got *their* parrot with his own unique qualities instead. In your parrot training, remember to accept reality and realize that you might have unfulfilled expectations. Don't give up on your bird, and don't start thinking that he isn't a fun companion because he is not learning a trick. Each bird is so special, you will find much to love in every bird, just give him a chance.

Chapter 2

Preparations for Training

This chapter will help you understand all the steps that are necessary before you start trick training your bird and also will answer many of your questions about actually training your bird. If you are seriously interested in teaching tricks to your parrot, he should be completely weaned and well socialized. That means if you are working with a young bird, he must be eating and drinking on his own, accept food from your hands, and be able to be touched all over. This would be number 5 or 6 on the Tameness Scale shown a bit later in this chapter. However, a bird of any age can be a good candidate for trick training if he meets these same requirements.

EARLY-BIRD TRAINING

Ideally, socialization will start during hand feeding, when a baby parrot is being raised as a companion bird and is taken from his parents to be raised by a person. The parrot chick is being trained every time he is handled. In fact, you are training the baby every time you pick him up. Every breeder or pet store that is feeding an unweaned parrot chick should be talking to him, handling him, and giving him lots of physical contact.

Obtaining a weaned parrot chick that has been well socialized during the hand-feeding process is the ideal for you, since you plan to train your parrot. But you can't always get a baby that the breeder or pet store has been able to handle that much. Start from wherever you are when you first get a baby. Handle and play with him as much as you can, emphasizing picking him up, touching his feet, holding his wings out, and feeding him treats by hand. If you are lucky enough to get a baby between the ages of 3 and 8 months, that is ideal. Parrots in the wild at that age would be learning from their parents and the other birds in a flock what they need to know just to survive. He would be learning his flock's calls, so

A well-socialized bird is a good candidate for trick training, such as this White-eyed Conure.

this is a great time to start teaching your bird to talk. He would be learning what to eat from foraging flockmates, so work on introducing the baby to all sorts of nutritious foods before food preferences become ingrained.

Aviculturists are learning the value of letting baby parrots fledge (fly) before going to their new homes and giving the new owners the choice of whether to clip their wing feathers or not. During a parrot's first few weeks of fledging, he learns to handle his body, land, and glide safely, as well as how to move about his environment. Letting the baby fly at this age has been shown to greatly increase a bird's self-confidence.

While the baby is learning about his environment, you should also teach him how to play, giving him toys and playing with the toys yourself, to show the baby how to play. Parrots learn by mimicking the behavior of their flockmates as well as learning vocalizations from them. It is a delightful inquisitive age when the baby is so trusting. But all babies grow up, and without proper guidance, they can turn into little monsters. It is up to you as a parrot caretaker to teach your youngster how to live in our world.

All baby parrots start out perfect; some of those we see in rescue facilities after moving from home to home are there because humans have let them down. My goal in writing this book is to give you some ideas on how to train these fragile

Bob Bartley acquired Gypsy thirty years ago and has built a wonderful bond of trust with his performing Scarlet Macaw.

beings, how to better communicate with them, and how to teach them what is expected of them in a human household. You will learn, at the same time, ways to interact with your bird and what you need to do to keep him happy. Hopefully, you and your bird will learn to respect each other. There's no better way to accomplish this than to start off by teaching your parrot something, like doing interesting tricks that you can both enjoy. When working with a parrot chick, start out slowly with short, fun sessions. As the baby matures (the age of maturity is from 6 months to 6 years, depending on the species of bird), you can start increasing the length of the training sessions and the difficulty of the behaviors or tricks.

TAMENESS SCALE

The following Tameness Scale is proposed by Kevin Murphy in his book, *Training Your Parrot* (T.F.H. Publications, 1983). Murphy emphasizes that this is a guide and is not intended as a blueprint for increasing tameness. Rather it shows how tameness may progress. But remember, each bird is an individual and will progress differently. So use this scale just as a guide to see where you are now with your bird and where you would like to go. It would be ideal if you and your bird were at least at number 5 before you start trick training.

1. The parrot will step from its cage to your hand, from one hand to the other, from your hand to its stand or cage, and will remain on your hand or the stand without jumping or flying off.

2. The bird allows you to touch his beak and rub his feet; he remains seated on your hand or wrist while you walk about.

3. Your companion bird allows you to touch his chest and facial feathers; will preen his feathers while seated on your hand; will play with a toy or eat a snack while seated on your hand; will walk up your arm and sit on your shoulder while you walk about; and will preen your hair and ears.

4. Your bird allows you to ruffle facial feathers and stroke the top of his head and neck. He hangs upside down from your fingers; sits on your shoulder,

and snuggles up to your face or will take a little catnap while you are hold-ing him; will sit on your hand and exercise his wings.

5. He allows you to ruffle feathers on the back of his neck, scratch his neck, stroke his back, cup your hand around his back, and grasp his tail feathers; hangs upside down from one hand and allows your other hand to support his back; allows you to gently swing him back and forth while he hangs from your hand by one or both feet; hangs from your fingers and beats his wings; performs other hand-to-hand acrobatics; allows you to hold him in both hands like a pigeon.

6. Your companion bird allows you to touch his body under his wings; will nestle down in your hands; will lie on his side or on his back, while his head may hang down looking about or be curled up preening leg feathers—will probably be holding your finger with one foot.

7. He allows you to spread his wings partway and ruffle his body feathers at the base of his tail, tummy, and legs; nestles down in your cupped hands and catnaps; allows toenails to be clipped and filed while sitting on perch.

8. The bird allows you to fully extend one wing to inspect feathers; allows you to probe and examine new feather growth while body feathers are fluffed up.

9. He allows you to fully extend both wings; will lie on his back in your cupped hands without holding on to you with its feet; will also lie in this position on your lap while you trim and file his toenails.

10. Your companion bird allows you to touch him any way you want without protest; allows you to clip his wing feathers while lying on your knee or seated on his stand.

ANY AGE BIRD CAN BE TRAINED

Your bird is never too old to learn. It is possible to train any parrot of any age, but training older birds will be more challenging than training babies. You might have to approach the training a little differently. From the time you first meet your new, older, or previously owned companion parrot, you are training him just by your interactions with him. It is important to work on building trust and reinforcing behaviors you like from your very first meeting. Work hard to learn his body lan-guage. You might be anxious to hold and cuddle your new pet, but let the bird tell you when he is ready for close interaction. At first, be satisfied when he takes food from your fingers without biting you. Be even happier if he is willing to step onto your hand or arm and let you carry him around. Older birds who have had many homes can bring a lot of baggage with them, so get to know your new bird well before you start any formal trick training.

There is no hurry, after all. With proper training, your parrot will be your lifelong companion. Start off with some of the easier requirements for trick training. Find out what his favorite food is. Work on being able to touch him all over his body. That can be a challenge, but it's essential in developing the trust needed for trick training. You might have to start out just holding a hand over your parrot or near him or touching him caressingly with a small stick that he will look at as an extension of your hand before he will actually let you touch him. Work in stages that are comfortable for your older parrot in order to build his trust and cooperation.

In order to make your parrot comfortable in many environments and situations, let him out of his cage as much as you can and take him to different parts of your house. Companion birds should become acclimated to change and variety in their surroundings. Introduce your parrot to the training table and T-stand perches that you will use in your training sessions (more on these later in the chapter). If you have already decided on the tricks you want to teach your parrot, let him see the props used for those tricks. Don't allow him to play with those props, but allow him to see them so he won't be afraid of them later. Give him many different toys to play with so he will be used to different shapes, colors, and sizes of objects in preparation for when you start seriously training him.

Talk to your parrot a lot so he will be used to the sound of your voice and know when you are happy and pleased with him. Of course, it is never too soon to work on his talking and mimicking speech (more in chapter 12, "Verbalizations and Talking"), or you might have adopted a parrot who knows a few words or phrases already. If your new bird has undesirable behaviors or speech, ignore them and start work at once on reinforcing the behaviors you do want.

THE TRAINING AREA

You will have the best success with your training if you choose a relatively quiet area, free from distractions, in which to train. Distraction-free applies to both you and your parrot. For your sake, there should be no ringing phones, noisy kids, or barking dogs to distract you from training. These same things can distract your bird too, of course, but more importantly the training area should be out of sight of the bird's own cage and away from other birds who might try to compete for your attention. But, if you don't have a distraction-free area in your home, make do with what you have and just get started.

After your bird understands what training is all about, then you may change the training area. Before that, try to be consistent by keeping the training area the same.

My first training place was a bathroom. It was the only room I could find where my bird and I wouldn't be interrupted or distracted. My training table was a folding TV tray. The first bird I trained was Poopsie, a little Green-cheeked Conure. As she progressed and learned some tricks I was eager to show her off to my friends.

But it was always a little embarrassing to have to ask my friends to come into the bathroom to see her perform!

Things have progressed. Now I have made the entire recreation room into a training room. My present training table is two feet by six feet with a plastic laminate top and a small lip around the edges of the table to prevent props like balls or scooters from accidentally rolling off. I can sit comfortably while training the bird, and the bird cannot get out of my reach. I don't worry about having the bird's head higher than mine. This might be a factor in working with a bird who has a behavior problem, but then one should not be trying to teach such a bird tricks until his other problems are solved.

TRAINING REWARDS FOR YOUR BIRD

The training method, called *positive reinforcement,* is the method used by almost all of today's professional trainers, whether they are teaching a bird, a dolphin, or an elephant. You can use this method, too, no matter what species of bird you are training or what trick you are trying to teach. The idea behind positive reinforcement is to immediately reward any behavior you are trying to shape (teach), and ignore any wrong moves or behaviors. The bird must have some reason to repeat a behavior, and the reward is the reason. Only behaviors that are rewarded in some way will be repeated.

As to what to use as a reward, take your clue from your bird. Does he really like to eat? Food is the most obviously recognized reward for most animals. With birds, seeds or nuts are usually a favorite, so start with those. To determine which seeds your bird likes best, present him with a variety of seeds in a dish and watch what he selects. Then narrow it down to just a few of the seeds he chooses first until you have his favorite. With this determined, do not offer your parrot that seed in regular feedings or for casual treats, but only give it to him from your hand while training.

Keep the treat small, something that can be quickly consumed and won't fill your bird up too fast. You can try offering little pieces of fruit; experiment and see what works best. Banana chips have been used, and they seem to work. However, if your bird is not a chowhound, maybe he will work for a scratch on the head, petting, and praise. Try different things, but remember a reward of some sort has to be given for your bird to repeat a behavior and, thus, learn what it is you are trying to teach.

Possible food rewards for your bird include banana chips, walnuts, peanuts, almonds, and sunflower or safflower seeds.

FOOD AS A TRAINING TOOL

Obviously a bird who has just eaten is not as apt to want a food reward as a bird who has not eaten recently. Withholding food is about motivation to receive a food reward. After eating a big Thanksgiving turkey dinner, we are not as eager for the pumpkin pie as we will be in an hour or so. Take that into consideration when training your parrot. The popular term for this aspect of training is *food deprivation*. That sounds so negative, but the idea behind it is not. Food rewards should be part of the total diet that a bird eats. A bird will be more eager to receive a food reward if he is a little hungry (not starved!). During natural periods in the day a bird eats, and also it is natural that a bird goes for some period each day without eating. What you want to do is schedule your bird's normal feedings around his training or show times.

If you train in the morning, don't give your bird his breakfast until after the training session. If you will have an evening show or lesson, serve your parrot dinner afterward. If you are going to be feeding your parrot many seeds or fatty nuts during the training session, be careful to eliminate such foods from his regular diet. After all, you really don't want an overweight, albeit highly trained bird. Definitely don't starve your bird. That just is not necessary and would be counterproductive.

I have seen some birds in shows that seemed to care only about how fast they could do a trick so they could get their food reward. It was obvious they were not having fun as they kept watching the treat cup all the time. That doesn't make for a good show or a happy bird. Balance your bird's food and treats so that he will receive a normal portion of healthy foods every day.

Squawk, my Blue-crowned Conure, is such a chowhound that I don't ever need to withhold food from her. She can eat her regular meals and still be eager for her treats. Cassie, my Black-headed Caique, is quite different. She loves the audience and performing so much that she will often ignore my proffered treat to run up to the front edge of the table and then run back and forth, hop, or bow to make the audience laugh or applaud. (What a ham!) That is her reward. Each bird is different, so use what best motivates your bird.

TRAINING SESSIONS

How long and how often should you and your parrot hold training sessions? No hard and fast rule exists. It depends strictly on you, the amount of time you have to spend, and your bird's response to training. Remember, teaching tricks is supposed to be fun; no time constraint or competitions exist with regard to learning a behavior. Training sessions offer you a wonderful time to play with your bird, a time for the two of you to get to know each other better and form a strong bond.

I will share what works for me regarding training sessions, but you need to adapt my advice to your situation and do what works for you and your birds. I hear and read so often that you should have several short training sessions rather than one long one. The reason is that supposedly the bird has a short attention span. The trainers who write these things evidently cannot hold their bird's attention for very long, so they recommend short sessions. But I don't have that problem. Trick training is supposed to be fun, and for me it is. I train my birds if and when I feel like it; I have no schedule, no time limits, and no self-imposed expectations. The result is happy birds eager to please and be with me.

Consider what happens when you stick to a rigid training schedule. You decide you are going to train your birds every day at 11 A.M. Maybe you do for a couple of weeks, but then inevitably another appointment comes up. Or maybe one day you just feel tired and not up to it. Your bird, on the other hand, has now become accustomed to having his lesson every day at 11 A.M. This is your special time together. Like most people, birds love routine. Our lives are not so unpredictable when we have a routine. But every so often we must miss a lesson, and as the newness of the training wears off, it seems like we have to miss a scheduled time a little more often.

Your bird doesn't understand this, and he becomes upset. Each bird seems to have his own way of showing it. Some pretend to forget what they just learned; others just appear to be less interested in the learning process; and some can get downright nasty when upset. On the other hand, if you have no set schedule, the bird is not disappointed if you don't show up at a particular time, but just happy and excited when you do come and have a lesson or play time together. Your bird knows that he is now going to receive your full attention and some special treats as well, so everything is win-win.

You want your parrot to know that you are the boss and that *you* decide when it is play or lesson time. If your bird works hard and you have fun together, probably the sessions will occur more often. Keeping the sessions fun is one of the reasons you won't have problems with a short attention span. A bird will be so eager for his time with you that you won't have to worry about keeping his interest. Contrast that with a short lesson two or three times a day every day, and the bird can get pretty burned out and not as eager.

Another reason for training at variable times is that sometimes you may be asked to have your bird perform. This is an honor. But if your bird is used to only being trained at 11 A.M., an evening show could be a problem. So plan ahead for when your bird is a star!

You can keep your bird's interest by keeping the pace of the lesson moving rather rapidly. As soon as your bird seems to grasp the idea of what you are teaching him, move on to something else. For instance, when you are teaching the *wave* and the bird finally gets the idea that all he has to do is lift his left foot to get his treat, move on. Don't bore your bird by having him repeat the same behavior over and over, hoping he will lift his foot a little higher, or maybe start to wave the foot. He will shortly lose interest, and then the trainer, rather than blaming herself, will

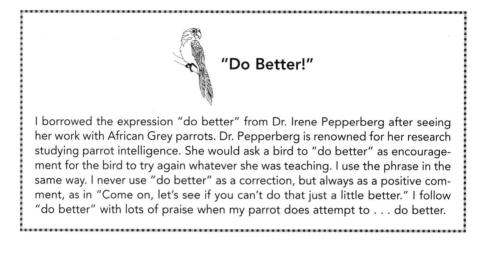

"Do Better!"

I borrowed the expression "do better" from Dr. Irene Pepperberg after seeing her work with African Grey parrots. Dr. Pepperberg is renowned for her research studying parrot intelligence. She would ask a bird to "do better" as encouragement for the bird to try again whatever she was teaching. I use the phrase in the same way. I never use "do better" as a correction, but always as a positive comment, as in "Come on, let's see if you can't do that just a little better." I follow "do better" with lots of praise when my parrot does attempt to . . . do better.

blame the bird's "short attention span." Instead, introduce something else to learn. Or do some socialization by gently tipping the bird onto his back or holding him aloft to flap his wings.

As a first lesson with your bird, you can introduce three tricks: the *turn around,* the *wave,* and the *shake hands* (all covered in chapter 5, "Tricks That Don't Require Props"). None of these tricks need to be taught to perfection, that can come later, but the concept for each is introduced, and you'll get excited each time the bird seems to grasp an idea. That in turn excites the bird and encourages him to try harder. The first lesson can easily run thirty to forty-five minutes. Chances are good you'll be ending the lesson with the bird still wanting more!

In his next lesson, whether the next day or the next week, your bird will remember everything learned in lesson 1 and will try to do even better.

If you find yourself losing patience or getting tired during a training session, quit while you're ahead. Quit on your terms; don't let your bird dictate when to stop training. If you feel you are really losing your bird's attention, switch to an easier trick, something he already knows for which you can praise and reward him. Then end the session. Take him back to his cage and again praise him and give him a special treat. Then leave him! Don't have a play session with your bird after a training session. You want the lesson to be his special time with you so he will look forward to just the training session. Keep play sessions separate.

HOW MANY TRAINERS?

You should be the only trainer for your bird as you begin working with him. You don't want your bird to become confused by different training methods or cues. After your bird has learned *how to learn* and what it means to be able to please his trainer, then a second person, after carefully watching what the first trainer does, could possibly also train the bird. It would be preferable, however, to have the second person teach a completely different trick, thus allowing your bird to get used to different training styles without too much confusion. Just have the second trainer take it slowly, and the bird will eventually catch on.

Despite my training experience with both birds and people, I sometimes have problems when I train a bird for someone else. I can show the owner what I do and what the bird has learned, but I find it is still very difficult for the bird to make a smooth transition to someone else. This problem seems to be unique to birds, as I did not have this problem when I was training dogs or horses.

TRIMMING WING FEATHERS

To trim or not to trim? That is the question. It's a personal decision and always a difficult one, whether to trim the wing feathers of a performing or companion bird. Trimming a bird's primary flight feathers will prevent him from flying or at least slow him down, but to trim or not becomes a yearly decision as flight feathers grow back at least that often. It is generally believed that leaving a baby's wings untrimmed until after he has fledged is best for the bird in order to develop his self-confidence and coordination. For trick training, though, after fledging, I do recommend you trim your bird's wing feathers so the bird will stay put on the training table. For doing shows it is almost a must, as no matter how well a bird is trained, you can never completely eliminate the *startle* reflex from a prey animal such as a bird.

Instinctive Response

After doing many shows, my birds are seasoned pros, and nothing much bothers them. They are used to audiences, kids yelling and coming up close to see them, sudden loud noises, flash bulbs going off, and lights and cameras in their faces. I live on a lake so I have big picture windows for them to see out of. They have gotten used to seeing all sorts of animals and birds, big and small; some even come around and peer in a window at them.

But one show I did that was outside was such a disaster that I have almost stopped accepting outdoor performances! In the middle of the show a hawk flew high overhead, and spotting us, made a circle and came back for a second look. I had four birds with me that day, three on their perches behind me and one on the table who was performing. The hawk was high in the sky, and neither I nor any of the people in the audience even noticed him. But all four of my birds almost simultaneously hit the ground and scattered. Luckily it was a bird-loving audience so my birds were all quickly scooped up and safely returned to their perches. But for the rest of the show my birds would take a quick look up into the sky to make sure everything was safe before they performed their next trick.

If you are the type who always remembers to close doors and windows, never leaves the toilet seat up, always stays in the kitchen to watch boiling pots, and doesn't mind the occasional unexpected bird poops or chewed furniture or window sills, then having a bird who can fly freely is a wonderful treat. Your bird will benefit from the exercise that flight naturally offers him. But, when you have a flighted companion bird (that is, one whose wing feathers have not been trimmed, and who can fly freely), you must also take responsibility for the potential that your beloved pet could fly out a door or a window or be carried outside should you forget he is on your shoulder. Work on the *come* command, described in chapter 4, "Necessary Obedience Skills (Husbandry Behaviors)," right away. You want to have some chance of getting an escaped bird back. In your work on the *come* command, be sure to include coming down from high places to your call. Many escaped companion birds have no concept of how to get down, from say a tall tree or wire, to an owner when they are outside.

If you do try to trick train an unclipped bird, you might want to start training in a small room with no furniture and no high places. Then after the bird has had some training and sees how much fun training can be, you can perhaps move to another room and still be successful.

However, if you have an aggressive bird who likes to attack people or pets, or is generally unfriendly, then it is advisable to clip the wing feathers. Again, this is a yearly decision, not a permanent life-long one. As you gain a bird's trust, you might decide to leave him flighted.

I attended a party at Naomi Zemont's on Bonney Lake, Washington, where many of the guests brought their fully flighted birds. I really enjoyed watching the birds have so much fun flying around, chasing one another off perches, and landing on different people who didn't seem to mind at all. I wished my birds could have joined them.

THE T-STAND

Before starting to trick train, have your training area all set up. Place a T-stand on the training table or use a floor model if you have a larger bird. You could leave your bird free on a table during training sessions, but you will have the most control and his undivided attention if he's sitting on a T-stand. A T-stand is a simple piece of equipment that consists of a flat base and an upright pole with a perch fastened perpendicular to the pole. This forms a "T" shape, hence the name. The size of the perch, of course, depends on the size of your bird. You can make a simple perch easily enough if you are handy with tools. All it takes to make a T-stand are a drill and saw. Directions for making this and other props are given in chapter 13, "Making Props." Many styles are also available from bird supply companies, bird stores, and bird catalogs. These range from portable stands to floor

Make sure your bird is comfortable in his training area and with his T-stand, either a table or a floor model.

models to tabletop versions. Do not use those stands that come with perches of various heights or that have play gyms or toys on them. These can become very distracting for your bird.

Take your bird to the training area and let him get used to his T-stand, the table, and the training props. Let him become comfortable with sitting on the T-stand and being handled before you start the actual training. Play with him there, gently tip him onto his back while holding him in your arms (don't put him on the table on his back yet, that will come later). Scratch him on his head and belly, touch his feet and under his wings. Your bird might not like being touched in certain areas, but do so gently anyway. You want him to see that he is not going to be hurt in any way, that hands are nice, and that hands also give him yummy treats. Pick him up with your hands over his back and again praise and feed him special treats. Let your bird see that this is a fun place to be. Then and only then are you ready to start formal training.

Chapter 3

Training Basics

You can train a behavior in many different ways. No one way is perfect for all parrots. What I will be showing in this book are ways that I know will succeed with most birds. Each trick I teach is actually one I have taught several birds, and I know the methods I suggest will work. Nothing is cast in stone, however, that says you have to teach a particular behavior in a certain way. Always be creative. Observe your bird carefully during the learning process and see what he seems to understand or where you might be confusing him. Changing the process slightly just might make a big difference. And never be in a hurry. Your bird might understand certain parts of a trick at once, but other parts might take a little longer to develop. Each bird will be different in the rate at which he learns. Usually it depends on what he has learned before. So go at your bird's rate. If a trick only takes one session, fine. If it takes two or three, that's fine, too and is no reflection on your bird's intelligence. The main thing is for you to have fun and make the experience enjoyable for both of you.

The following terms describe methods commonly used in training. You will encounter these terms as well as others in your training.

TARGETING

Targeting is a very useful behavior and is a basic foundation skill. It is sort of a trick in itself, but its real use is in helping teach some of the more complex behaviors. Targeting means that your bird will follow a target, and touch it when you ask him to.

The most commonly used targets are *target sticks* or even your hand. The target stick can be any of a variety of objects. The target stick does not have to be very long since your bird will be working close to you on a stand or the training table. A chopstick, a wooden dowel, or even a knitting needle can be used. If you want to use a wooden dowel, just make sure you never use that particular dowel later as a perch or it could really confuse the bird.

Make the end of your chosen target stick, the part you want the bird to touch, a different color. You can do this by wrapping a piece of colored tape around one end, or if the target stick is wood, dipping one end in some nontoxic food coloring. Your goal is to teach your bird to touch the end of the stick with his beak. Hold the stick somewhere in front of your bird's face and ask him to "touch." Very often the bird will out of curiosity reach for the target stick. Praise and reward (or P&R, as I will refer to it throughout the book) your bird immediately. Do not let him chew on the target stick, only reward his touching it. Resist the urge to touch your bird's beak with the stick. He must actively reach to touch the stick himself to get his reward.

For the rare bird who just ignores the target stick, move it around a little bit, but not so aggressively as to frighten him. If he still ignores it, try a little peanut butter on the end, or jelly, or something you know your bird likes. Don't let him chew on the stick; the enhancement is there only to get him interested in it. Let the treat/reward come from you. He will very soon get the idea of touching the target stick to get his reward. Then move the stick around the table so he has to walk to touch it. If he is on a floor perch, hold the target stick to first one side, then the other, and even hold it behind him to make him turn around and reach for it. Use your cue word "touch" until he will reliably go for the stick any time he sees it. Be enthusiastic. Remember, tricks are meant to be fun for both you and your parrot. Be aware of your pet's safety and physical limitations at all times.

This is usually a very easy behavior to teach. You might be able to teach this in one session, or it might take you a few sessions depending on you and your bird. Once learned, you can use the behavior to teach other behaviors such as the *turn around,* stepping on to a handheld perch, or going to an unfamiliar prop.

SHAPING A BEHAVIOR

You train a parrot to perform a trick behavior by teaching small pieces of the finished trick. This is called *shaping*. Break the behavior you want to teach into small successive steps. Teach your bird to perform one small easy-to-accomplish step and reward him for doing it. Then withhold his reward for performing this first step and raise your requirements for the reward. In his attempts to get another reward, your bird will usually try harder to do whatever he thinks you want. Usually one of the attempts will be a closer approximation to the finished behavior you are working toward and so can be P&R'd. Then up the ante again. And again the parrot will try to do something that he hopes will get him that treat. One of the varied attempts will be even closer to the final trick and so can be P&R'd. You reward only the appropriate responses and ignore the rest. The rewarded responses will be the ones repeated.

Soon, by these small easy steps, you will have the finished behavior. These small steps are often referred to as "baby steps." The number of steps needed and the size of the steps depend on the difficulty of the trick and the training experience of both you and your bird. This method uses a concept called *partial extinction;* see the explanation later in this chapter.

PHYSICAL ASSISTANCE (MOLDING)

Physically handling your bird and helping him through training steps is perfectly acceptable but depends mainly on the relationship you have with your bird. If you are able to pick him up, with your hands over his back, turn him over onto his back, cuddle him, and so on as described in chapter 4, "Necessary Obedience Skills (Husbandry Behaviors)," then physically manipulating your bird should not be a problem. (This level of socializing falls at number 5 on the Tameness Scale mentioned in chapter 2, "Preparations for Training".) Teaching your bird to lie on his back, roll over, stand on his head, and so on is so much easier when you can physically assist him to do so. These tricks, of course, can be taught using a target stick and luring with rewards, but don't be afraid to physically, always gently, help your bird to the correct position. Once shown what he is supposed to do, it usually takes very little time before your bird is doing the trick on his own.

LURING

Luring is another teaching method akin to bribing, but the term luring sounds better. It is a method used to entice a parrot to do something. A lure is any object that will retain the bird's attention. Food is usually the best lure. You can increase your chances for successful luring by having a hungry bird and a wonderful food treat. If I want to lure a bird to a new prop, I might place his treat next to or under the prop to get him to go investigate the prop. If the bird suddenly forgets what he is supposed to do, then shaking his treat cup should get his attention and cause him to refocus. I have used luring to teach several of the tricks in this book, such as getting a bird to climb a ladder or a rope. I hold the bird's treat at the top of the ladder where he can see it and "lure" him into climbing to the top to get it.

I also use luring in one of the first tricks I teach, when the bird is first learning how to learn and learning what this training is all about. With the bird on the T-stand, I hold his treat in front of his face and get him to follow my hand with the treat to turn around and face back, where he gets his treat. Then I lure him to turn the rest of the way around by following the treat until he faces front again. As the bird learns the *turn around,* the lure is gradually faded out and just the hand moving in a circle above the bird's head is kept as the cue.

These are legitimate teaching methods, but as in most cases of luring, you probably also could use a target stick just as well to reach your desired goal.

CAPTURING A BEHAVIOR

As parrot trainers we do not create a behavior. We simply use behaviors that a parrot already knows how to do. Choosing from the behaviors your parrot already does, and through shaping and rewarding, you train your parrot to perform a trick behavior on cue. Some behaviors your parrot offers are so cute you do not want to change a thing; you only want to "capture" the behavior as is and put it to a cue. These *innovative behaviors* can lead to some of the best tricks your bird might perform. Examples would be a parrot's hopping, stretching his wings, bobbing his head, and many more that can be specific to a particular bird or species. These are such fun behaviors, I have devoted chapter 10, "Innovative Tricks," to discussing these tricks and how to "capture" them.

CLICKER TRAINING

Other types of training methods can be used when training your bird—for example, using a clicker. A *clicker* is a little metal box that makes a clicking sound when pressed. The clicker takes its name from the little metal crickets kids used to play with that made a clicking sound. It is used as a bridge, which is a signal, that tells the bird being trained that he is doing a desired behavior correctly and to "bridge" the gap between that moment and when he will actually be rewarded. Any sound, word, or phrase can be used as a bridge. When working with dolphins and other sea life, a police-type whistle is often used because it can be heard under water and carries a long distance. When working with sheepherding dogs, the dog might be working independently at some distance, so the master whistles to give his dog signals. I have also heard of a laser pointer, or even a flashlight, being used effectively with some special types of training. A clicker is sometimes used when training dogs in agility exercises, although it can't be used in final competitions.

The clicker has recently become popular for bird training among a certain group of devotees. The theory is that you use the clicker sound to tell your bird two things: exactly and at what point he has performed the correct behavior and to act as a bridge to tell him a reward will be forthcoming. The disadvantages are that you must continually carry this metal clicker around with you, and the click will stop the action. Your parrot is supposed to stop whatever he is doing when he hears the sound and come to you for his reward. Also it adds another step to the training process. Your bird has to be taught what the click means, which is a lesson in itself. Even die-hard clicker trainers will tell you they drop the clicker and go to verbal praise after a trick is learned. So why do they need a clicker to start with?

You Don't Need to Use a Clicker

You don't need to add clicker training to your repertoire to become a good trainer. It's an extra step that really slows your training down. I have had clicker trainers say that training with a clicker is faster. I really challenge that premise. I have tested it, and I know it slows you down. If you need to mark an exact moment in your bird's training, you can say "good" just as fast and with the exact timing needed, as someone else can click a little metal box. I can't think of a single trick where this would be an advantage, especially when you are training a bird who is right in front of you on the table or T-stand where a reward can be given at the same time as the praise. No bridge is needed because no time gap exists between the correct action and the reward. You can give your bird his treat with lots of praise, immediately.

A training video currently on the market shows someone trying to train a behavior that takes some physical manipulation. The person finally realized he couldn't handle the prop, the parrot, the treat, and the clicker all at once. So he handed the clicker to someone else and asked him to please do the clicking for him when the bird performed the desired behavior. How ridiculous. And it shows it right on the video! Now you have to have two people to train your bird?

Your bird has heard your voice from the time you first got him. That is your big advantage. So use it. Your bird has heard you telling him many times what a good bird he is. He knows from the tone of your voice whether you are pleased or not or when you are excited by his behavior. You don't have to teach him that as a separate lesson, either. Let a clicker try to tell your bird that you are pleased with him.

And unlike clicker training where the click immediately stops the action, and the bird expects the reward to be forthcoming before continuing on with the trick, I use my voice and generally a whole phrase containing the word "good," like "good bird" or "good baby" or "that was good," to tell my bird that he is doing it right and to encourage him to continue the behavior. I don't want him to stop the action. This is true whether I am asking him to ride a bicycle, climb a ladder, or perform some antic I think is worth saving and could possibly be made into an innovative trick (see chapter 10). When the behavior is finished I reward him and encourage him to try it again and maybe do it just a little better. You never want to stop the action in the middle of teaching a trick just to give your bird a treat for doing something.

I use the standard conventional method that is now popularly called the "positive reward" method of trick training. Clicker training enthusiasts like to say that the conventional way of using a praise word, in my case "good" or some form of it, makes that method the same as the clicker method, just substituting a word for the click. It's not the same at all! My "good" or similar words of praise do not stop the action but merely tell the bird he is doing what I want. My main P&R comes immediately after the action is finished. In my case, the action could be a chain of tricks performed together in one skit. I use my voice to give my birds praise and encouragement while they are performing.

Remember what I am saying here applies only to training parrots who are on a T-stand or a table right in front of you. It does not apply to dolphins, dogs, or other animals who can be at a distance from the trainer, or are not pets, such as the chickens who I once trained using the clicker method. I do use a verbal and a visual cue right from the beginning. True clicker trainers say they prefer to add the cues after the trick is learned. Again, that is just adding another unnecessary step.

Comparing the Positive Reward Method to Clicker Training

I'll give you an example of the differences between the two methods. Let's say you are teaching the *wave* using a clicker. You must wait until your bird offers to shift weight or somehow move his left foot. You click and treat (abbreviated CT) and then you wait until your bird offers to do so again. After many pairings, your bird maybe has learned that when he lifts his left foot slightly he gets a click and a reward. This is repeated many times to make sure that your bird understands the connection.

With the positive reward method I use, I start by waving my right fingers at the bird in small wave motions and saying "wave," then presenting my left hand in front of his left leg as though asking for a step up. The bird starts to lift his leg to step onto me. I quickly withdraw my hand and P&R. You get an immediate response from the bird, and the first step is accomplished. I don't have to wait for the bird to offer the action. A few more times, and the bird will be tentatively lifting his leg in response to my command and signal. It took all of about ten minutes for the bird to show he had an understanding of the trick. How long for the clicker trainer to even get his bird to offer the behavior and then how much longer before he could add a verbal or physical cue?

A bridge signal to mark a correct response and to fill the "time gap" between a behavior and the reward is unimportant, which was illustrated when I attended a weeklong clicker training class given by Bob and Marion Bailey (prior to her death) at their chicken training camp in Arkansas. We were instructed how to offer the treat to a chicken at the same time we clicked to signal the proper behavior. The treat cup and the clicker were both on the same foot and a half stick that we held out to the chicken on the table in front of us. I found it didn't make a bit of difference whether we clicked or not. Believe me, I really experimented with this proposition. Since the chicken was not my pet and couldn't have cared less whether I praised her or was pleased, I soon dropped the praise part of my method. The chicken responded only to seeing the treat cup and getting her reward. Whether you clicked or not made absolutely no difference. But with our own pet parrots, I really believe that they do respond to our petting and praise and will sometimes work for just that. A chicken won't, and many other animals won't work for praise alone, either.

Real Life Training

Using a clicker, a whistle, or artificial sound is very effective with animals you don't touch when training, or who don't care to be touched, or who are working some distance from their trainer. Dolphins would be an excellent example, or the crows trained by Keller Breland. My friend Stan Kramien, who worked with ponies in the show ring, said the clicker was the main way to communicate with the ponies. In the show ring, he cracked a whip to signal changes in direction, speed, and so on. But in the training arena, he used a clicker. I asked him why he didn't use a clicker when he trained his parrots for his bird act. He answered that he didn't need to since the birds were always right in front of him, within reach.

I always have my voice with me. I can't imagine, when my bird is trying to say a new word, having to go find the clicker so I can let her know she is doing well. My voice can tell her that immediately, even from the next room, that I hear her, that I like what she is trying to say, and that I think she is pretty wonderful. Let a clicker try to do that.

I read a book recently by a prominent clicker trainer who was describing how you would teach a bird to ride a bicycle. To begin teaching the trick, he said he was going to assume that you were starting with a bird with a strong hunger or treat drive . . . and that the bird would stop any activity instantly when he heard the sound of your clicker, expecting to receive food from your hand or on the training table. He suggests you begin by placing the bicycle at the end of the train- ing table and then place a small quantity of food around the rear wheel of the bike. When your bird picks up a seed or two, you sound your clicker and place a seed on the table in front of you as you require your bird to come to you for the rein- forcement. As soon as your bird approaches and takes the food, reward him. You put more food down by the bike just a bit closer. Then you wait until the bird eats that food and you again immediately CT. Reward for several trials. You keep mov- ing the food closer and closer to the bike. You are essentially shaping your bird's behavior as you get him to move nearer and nearer your goal of going directly to the bike. He says this may be the only progress you make during the first session.

The author goes on to say that by lesson three he wants the bird to get the idea that the rewards are somehow connected to the bicycle so that he goes to the bicy- cle and expectantly waits there. In lesson four, after much trial and error, he expects the bird to maybe put his foot on a part of the bike and then maybe climb onto the back wheel. In lesson six (he calls it step six, as he says you may have to go back and repeat steps so it could take more than that number of lessons), he asks the bird to put his feet on the pedals. That's it for that lesson. And so it goes. Each time you click the action is stopped; the bird has to leave the bicycle and go to his trainer to get his treat. This process is called "shaping." Shaping a behavior in little incre- ments can be very effective, but good heavens, with the conventional method I would have had the bird already peddling down the table. You will see when we get to my section on teaching bicycle riding in chapter 9, "Miscellaneous Tricks."

I will drop the subject now, but just don't let anyone try to tell you that clicker training is easier or faster. Take it from someone who has tried both ways and knows. I can show you how to train a parrot any behavior more quickly and more efficiently without a clicker!

OPERANT CONDITIONING

Now let's discuss some of the terms that are commonly used by animal trainers. Operant conditioning is the process that happens whenever any creature performs a behavior and then learns from the consequences of its actions. When the consequences are something that is liked, then the behavior is likely to be repeated. We say that the behavior has been positively reinforced. When the consequences of the behavior is something disliked, then the behavior is less likely to be repeated. Punishment falls into this category. And when nothing happens as a direct consequence of the behavior, then the behavior is likely to cease to be offered. Behaviorists call this *extinction,* as I'll explain next.

Operant conditioning suggests that learning is predictable, that it is governed by laws, and that the underlying process of learning is basically the same for all creatures: mice, humans, dogs, birds, or whatever. Operant conditioning is a learning theory that focuses on the consequences as the controlling factors for behavior. Every behavior has an antecedent, something that precedes the behavior and causes the behavior. Then every behavior has a consequence, something that comes after the behavior. The type of consequence, whether pleasant or unpleasant, determines how likely it is that the behavior will be repeated. If we were speaking in these terms, we would say the bird received a "reinforcement" for the correct behavior instead of a reward. And to follow this up, every reward becomes reinforcement, but not every reinforcement is a reward.

The way I will be using the term *reward* in this book means something the bird likes, finds pleasurable, and will work to receive. The universal reward for most animals is food. But if your bird absolutely does not care about food treats, then use head scratches, praise, or anything else your bird will work for. Punishment or harsh methods have no place in parrot training and should never be used.

In operant conditioning terms, *trick behaviors* are really just conditioned behaviors. You have conditioned your bird to respond to your cues.

PARTIAL EXTINCTION

It has been found that when a given behavior is not rewarded in some way for the bird, that eventually the behavior will cease. But before it does, the bird has what has been termed an extinction burst. That is, the behavior temporarily increases, before the bird gives up, so to speak, and the behavior ceases. This concept is what we are using in shaping and taking baby steps in our training. The bird is no longer receiving a reward for what he was doing previously and in frustration tries even harder to do something more to get that reward. In doing so, he inadvertently usually takes that next step toward the desired trick and so immediately gets P&R. This is what is meant by partial extinction. The behavior is not eliminated completely, or extinguished, but just the one part the bird was doing is replaced by another behavior closer to the final goal. In other words, the transition through the training steps of a shaping sequence involves the alternate application of reward and partial extinction.

CUES: VERBAL AND PHYSICAL

I use the term *command* as just another term for a verbal cue. It is not meant in the military sense of a strong or strident order. If I say the command for this trick is "dead bird," it just means that is the verbal cue I suggest you say and has nothing to do with how you say it.

A cue can be either physical or verbal. In other words, it's a visible or an audible signal that a parrot can see or hear. A cue is used to tell or signal your bird what he is supposed to do. In many of the behaviors I will tell you to use both while you are teaching the trick. But once learned, one or the other cue can be dropped. Since birds are very visually oriented, it is usually the verbal cue that can be dropped. Cues can be very obvious or very subtle—your choice after the trick is learned. In many cases with prop tricks, the presence of the prop is enough to signal the behavior to follow and neither a verbal nor physical cue is needed. An example would be presenting your bird with a basketball and the basketball hoop. By association your bird knows to pick up the ball and put it in the hoop. You don't have to tell him to pick up the ball and then show him where to place it. Another good example is presenting your bird with your hand, arm, or a hand-held perch and then saying "step up." Your hand is the "prop," so to speak, so you do not need to give a command to "step up."

However, in teaching your bird to talk on cue, it is almost always a verbal cue you use. If your bird is already saying his name, for example "Charlie," you get him to repeat the word after you say it and P&R. You only P&R when he says it after you and not when he randomly offers it. Then you add your cue word of "name." You say "name" and then "Charlie." When he says "Charlie" after you, P&R. Always pair your cue word with the desired answer. Soon you will be able to drop saying his name, and he will respond with his name when he hears the cue word of "name." Then you can add all the talk you want, asking him to give you his name, or saying "Have you got a name?" or whatever you want, as long as you end with the cue word "name."

I will be giving you cues you can use with each trick, but they are only suggestions that have worked for me. You can use whatever cues work for you. As long as you are consistent, use whatever cue is easiest for you. Just be sure the cue, whether verbal or physical, is not too similar to any another cue you use for

Pretty Bird

When I do a talking part in my show, I sometimes ask my bird, Squawk, after she tells me her name, if she is an ugly bird or a pretty bird. She was saying "pretty bird" early on, so I tried to figure out a way I could incorporate the phrase into the show. I came up with the lame idea I just mentioned. Anyway, she soon figured out what I was saying and what she was supposed to answer. I would just start to ask the question, "Are you an ugly bird?" and before I could finish the sentence she would cut me short and answer "Pretty bird." I would tell her to wait for the cue and not reward her, but her answer always made the audience laugh so I gave up and decided to do it her way; from then on, I rewarded her for the interruption, only pretending to be annoyed, and made it a part of the show.

another trick. You don't want to confuse your bird with mixed signals. And if you are planning to always use a cue for a particular behavior, be sure you never reward your bird if the behavior is offered without the cue being given.

GENERALIZING

One of the most wonderful things about teaching parrots tricks is their ability to generalize—to apply what they have learned in one situation to another situation. I will be emphasizing this over and over again when teaching the *retrieve* in upcoming chapters. More than any other single behavior, the *retrieve* can be the basis of so many other tricks, just because of the parrot's ability to generalize. In the *retrieve*, you have taught your bird to bring you whatever object you ask for and to place it in your hand or wherever else you may designate. This leads to the bird then generalizing the concept to understand it also applies to bringing you a ring to place on a peg, a coin to put in a piggy bank, a ball to put in a basketball hoop, or a grocery cart to fill up with groceries. How about putting a baby in a baby buggy, and then taking the baby from the buggy and putting it into a cradle? These tricks all involve taking an object from one place and putting it in another. Just think if you had to teach each behavior separately. But with the parrot's ability to generalize, you can move easily from one trick to another.

Chapter 4

Necessary Obedience Skills (Husbandry Behaviors)

Hopefully you and your parrot will have many years together. If you have adopted a young bird, the chances are he may even outlive you. The time to teach good husbandry skills is when you first bring your bird home to live with you, before any bad habits get a chance to form. So what are husbandry skills, and how do you teach them? Husbandry skills are behaviors you expect from your bird in everyday living situations, and teaching them isn't very different from teaching tricks. The same patience, goals, and rewards that you use in teaching tricks can be employed when teaching husbandry skills.

Think about when you first brought a new puppy home. The most important things were to potty train him, show him where his food dish was and where he was to sleep, perhaps crate train him, and teach him not to jump up on the furniture or your bed, and what his name was and to come when called. This was not considered trick training, but teaching necessary obedience commands.

So it is with your new parrot. He must be introduced to his cage and taught to stay there by himself. He will have to find his food and water dishes. He must be taught to come out of his cage when asked and to politely step onto your hand. Then your bird should allow himself to be carried to another perch or place and to remain quietly in that place until removed. He should be taught to hold out a foot for nail trimming and a wing for wing clipping if that is desired. Eventually he can even be potty trained. Most people wouldn't call these tricks, even though they involve training. These aren't the kind of tricks you use to show off your bird's cleverness, but they increase the satisfaction of living with him exponentially. These behaviors we like to classify as husbandry behaviors, and learning them will make life safer, more fun, and more stimulating for you and your parrot.

STEP UP

Probably the first skill you'll try to teach your bird, if he hasn't already learned it, is to step onto your hand or wrist. It is much easier to transport your bird on your hand or arm than to grasp your bird with both hands around his body, like you would carry a chicken.

When possible, I like to start teaching the *step up* when first hand-feeding a baby. I am an experienced hand feeder, so I occasionally get to hand-feed parrot chicks. I have hand-fed just about all of my present performing birds. However, if you are not experienced at doing this, leave it to the experts and get a chick that is already weaned. It will make little difference in your final pet parrot. But here is what I like to do when I get the chance to hand-feed a baby. After the baby settles in and gets to recognize me as "mama," I hold the syringe or the spoon I am using to feed him a soft, warm parrot formula, and call the baby to come. When the baby toddles to me to get his formula, he has just had his first lesson. As the baby grows, I might place my hand on the table and let the baby climb onto it to be fed. As soon as the baby can perch, I turn my hand so that he is now stepping or climbing onto my finger. This is an easy way to train the *step up*. I use the command *come* to give the dual meaning to the command, not only to step up onto my hand but also to come to me to step up. In the meantime I am also holding the baby, playing with his feet, turning him over in my hands, touching him under the wings, and so on. By the time the baby is fully weaned, he has been well socialized, too.

It is becoming increasingly common in the United States to be able to purchase well-socialized companion birds. More breeders, pet stores, and bird owners are recognizing the delight of owning a socialized baby bird. The days of the wild caught birds are practically over. Few birds have been imported into the United States since the Wild Bird Conservation Act was enacted in 1992. Even rescued birds have usually had some training in the *step up* concept. But for the bird that has not been previously trained to step onto a hand, here is one way to proceed.

Take your new bird to a restricted area, away from his cage and other birds, to teach this important concept. That means no other people around as well. Any small room will do. There should be no tempting heights that the flighted bird could possibly escape to,

Lucy, a female Solomon Island Eclectus, is learning to step from perch to perch.

and you should be able to close the door. I take my bird to a well-lighted hall, which I can close off from the rest of the house, and that has no place up high for a bird to perch on. I sit on the floor with my bird and talk soothingly to him until he seems fairly calm. I like to teach the bird to get on a stick/perch first, mainly to keep from getting bitten (it's always a possibility) and because it is important later to have the bird be able to accept alternate perches.

I place two sticks on the floor near him and let him see them and get used to them. Sometimes the bird will even step on one and use it as a perch. I give him any special treat I think he may like to eat. Then I place one stick slowly under his belly, low in front of his legs and ask him to "come," the command I use. Sometimes I use a treat held in front of the stick to encourage him to step onto the stick and get the treat. Usually the bird will do so with little resistance. I give lots of praise at this point and, of course, give him a treat. If you do have a bird who is flighted or if you are afraid he might try to escape, the enclosed hallway where there is no place for him to go is ideal. If he does try to fly away, with no where to go, he will just end up back on the floor with you. Keep talking soothingly to him and coaxing him to take a treat. Then try again. It doesn't take long before he will be tentatively standing on the stick. Lift it just a few inches and stop again. Offer him a treat again. If he moves to bite the hand that is holding the stick while he is perched on it, distract his attention with your free hand.

Next I hold the other stick in front of him and encourage him to step up onto it. Remember, birds find it easy to step up onto something and difficult to step lower then their body position. So always hold the stick in such a way that they can step up easily onto it. "Ladder" him by having him step from one stick onto the other in succession until he can do so easily. Don't hurry him. Let him set the pace. Each little advance is an accomplishment. Take plenty of time and make sure he is calm before proceeding to the next step.

If all goes well start substituting your finger, hand, or arm, depending on the size of the bird, for the bird to step onto. Place the stick on the floor and let him step onto your hand. Hold your hand on edge, fingers extended close together, with the thumb tucked into your palm. You may have observed that your bird tests each new perch with his open beak before he steps on. Don't panic when he does the same thing to your hand. If his beak starts to squeeze, say "gentle" and roll your hand toward your body to disengage the beak. Don't pull away. You must trust the bird as you expect him to trust you. If you shy away as soon as you feel his beak, he will not consider you a reliable perch. Then you will really have trouble getting him to step onto your hand. Watch him carefully, especially if he seems at all afraid of your hands or inclined to challenge you and bite. In this case, keep a stick in your other hand and use it to distract him and deflect the potential bite. Never, I repeat, *never*, hit the bird. The other stick is used only when necessary to

Left: Proper placement of finger in front of chest of pearl Cockatiel Daniel. Right: Daniel demonstrates laddering, stepping from one finger to another.

distract him. After the bird sees he is not being harmed and is rewarded and praised for stepping up peacefully, he will usually do so readily.

The next step is to ladder him from hand to hand until he is comfortable with this procedure. Finally, stand up with the bird on your hand. Move around with him and let him get used to the movement. When he seems comfortable, open the door to the hallway and walk around with him, talking to him constantly. Do not go within sight of his cage! Take him to a standing perch and ask him to transfer to that perch with the command *perch*. Then ask him to step onto your hand again with the command *come*. Always give the *come* command in a light happy voice to help convince the bird that to go with you is going to be fun.

COME AND PERCH

I use the *come* and the *perch* commands instead of the *up* or *down* command commonly advocated because I want the commands to have dual meanings for the bird right from the beginning. *Come* means to come to me from wherever, and *perch* means to go to a designated perch, not just step down onto a perch that is right in front of him. The *step up* command becomes redundant after a while when the physical cue of your hand is right in front of the bird. The same with the *step down* command when the place, cage, or wherever you want him to transfer to is right in front of him. You don't need a verbal cue if the physical cue is always present. Try it sometime. We get in the habit of always saying "step up" when presenting our hand to our bird. The trained bird will just as readily climb onto our hand whether we say "up" or not. What I want the bird to learn is the *come* command, which also means to come from the back of the cage, or from across the table, or from wherever he is when he is called, to my hand. As your parrot's training advances, his thorough training in the *come* command at this time will make "recall training" from a distant perch, his cage, or a high tree already mostly trained. You will just be adding distance to an already-learned concept. The same with the *perch* command. He is to go to wherever you designate, whether another perch, the training table, or his cage. He must also learn to be able to step up or down to this new perch. For instance the training table surface can actually cause him to have to step down from your hand, instead of up onto another perch. In his more advanced training, "perch" can take on the added meaning of actually flying to a designated spot or perch.

STAY

I teach the *stay* command much like I used to teach it to my dogs. I place the bird on the training T-stand or a floor perch, both of which are higher than a regular table perch. The main consideration is that the bird should not be tempted to just hop off the stand easily. Believe it or not, my commands and cues are exactly those I used with my dogs. I just drop my hand in front of the bird's face, palm facing the bird, and say "stay." I wait just a few moments and then give the release command of *okay* and give praise and reward (P&R). Gradually increase the time the bird must wait for the release *okay*. At first the bird is probably too confused to do

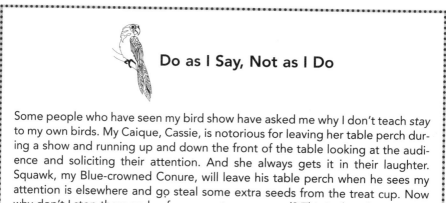

Do as I Say, Not as I Do

Some people who have seen my bird show have asked me why I don't teach *stay* to my own birds. My Caique, Cassie, is notorious for leaving her table perch during a show and running up and down the front of the table looking at the audience and soliciting their attention. And she always gets it in their laughter. Squawk, my Blue-crowned Conure, will leave his table perch when he sees my attention is elsewhere and go steal some extra seeds from the treat cup. Now why don't I stop them and enforce my *stay* command? This is show biz, and the audience thinks it's great when my birds seem to get the better of me. So I let them do it. They both have been taught the *stay* command, but when you don't enforce a command, these intelligent creatures are quick to take advantage, and I simply allow them to do it as part of our act.

anything else but sit there, but eventually he'll get the idea he wants to leave and not wait for a release command. If he does, put him back on the stand and do not give any treats. When he stays on the stand until released, he gets lots of P&R. As your bird becomes more willing to *stay,* slowly increase the amount of time he is asked to stay put, and finally, the acid test, leave the room briefly. This "trick" has to be repeated many times before there is any real reliability; birds simply don't understand when you leave the room that there is any necessity for them to *stay.*

GO TO YOUR CAGE

Some birds are cage bound and don't want to come out of their cages, and some, once out, don't want to go back into their cages! First we're going to discuss that important husbandry behavior of your bird—going back into his cage when asked. While working on this behavior, I would limit all feeding of your bird to inside his cage. I know various tree-type perches have feeding cups on them, but you don't have to use them, except maybe for water. I'm not talking about treats and things like that; I'm referring to your bird's regular diet. Keep it within the confines of his cage. A bird's regular diet includes his seeds, pellets, fruits, and veggies, as well as people food you feed your bird every day. Do not have them available at various stands or places around the house. His food must always be in his cage if you want to train this behavior.

After your bird will reliably go to his cage on direction, you can feed him wherever you like. Cage-only feeding is strictly a training tool. When you have finished a training or a play session with your bird, return him to inside his cage and give him special treats when he is inside, and then leave him. You can return later and let him out of his cage to sit on top of it, but when you go back later, only give him treats when he is inside his cage. Go by his cage frequently when he is inside it to talk with him and offer treats and maybe a head scratch while he is inside. Also make sure he has plenty of toys and things to do when he is inside the cage. The command is simply "get in your cage" said in a light happy voice and then place a treat or something else he might like, like a favorite toy or a new toy, inside the cage for him to see. Do not use his cage as punishment or a place for a time out at this time.

All you want your bird to do is go willingly into his cage when asked. My birds are out of their cages most of the day, so when nighttime comes they head into their cages of their own accord. If your bird sleeps in his cage, use this occasion to go to him just a little early, while he is outside his cage, and ask him to "get into your cage." Since it is something he probably wants to do anyway, he will undoubtedly comply, and you can P&R. Keep up the combination of asking him to go to his cage and lots of P&R when he does, and it does not usually take too long before your pet will be happy to do as asked.

Lucy going into her cage peacefully using the perch method.

When teaching this behavior, practice taking him to his cage often, sometimes putting him inside and then taking him right out again, sometimes putting him on a perch inside his cage, leaving him for a short amount of time, and then asking him to come out again. You want to keep him off guard so he will not always know what you are going to do. Always, of course, give him lots of P&R when he readily goes into his cage. However, if your bird is usually locked up for the day, when he is asked to return to his cage, he will be much more reluctant to comply.

POTTY TRAINING

Most people don't realize how easy it is to potty train their bird. Your bird is never going to fly to you or say "I have to go the bathroom, please," but you can with a little time and effort teach him to "go" in a designated place. Here's how.

Do wait until your pet is physically mature to start serious potty training. The ability to do this trick, for most birds, can be anywhere from 6 months to 1 year of age. Use a verbal cue that will not embarrass you if your bird says it in polite company. My cue words are "hurry up." My bird or I can use it at any time without attracting comment. First select an area or place where you want the bird to defecate. Do you want it to be a specific place like your pet's cage or play stand, or do you want your bird trained to respond to a cue word so that you can move the "potty place" around with you as a newspaper or a wastepaper basket? If your bird flies or can get to his cage or play stand on his own, then perhaps the cage or a stand would be the best place to use. You could wait before taking him out of his cage in the morning, giving your cue of "hurry up," until he "goes," and then take him out of his cage. Remember, birds have a very short retention span and will need to defecate every twenty minutes or so—a shorter time for smaller or younger birds, a little longer for larger birds.

Watch your bird carefully for the physical signs he gives when he needs to relieve himself. He will usually give some sort of signal when he needs to "go." Some birds squat and shake their tails; some stay still with a fixed stare; others run around nervously. Each bird is different, so learn to read your bird and what his signals are.

Start timing the frequency at which your bird needs to "go." No bird is able to wait indefinitely, so unless your bird can get to his potty place by himself, you are the one who will have to be trained. For your shoulder bird, you will just have to watch the clock and take him to a designated spot or hold him over a newspaper. Use the command "hurry up." Continue to hold your bird over the paper until he finally "goes." Then P&R. Each time you will find the bird "goes" a little more quickly as he begins to understand what you want. This is as close

Now, where's the toilet paper?

to potty training as you can get for the nonflighted bird. But if he is on your shoulder, and you don't remember to take him to the designated area, he will "go" on you. Since I have my birds on my shoulder a lot, and I can never remember to let them relieve themselves every fifteen minutes or so, I have lots of accidents on me. I rectify the problem by just changing shirts often. If you're concerned about poops on your clothes, there are commercially available covers for your clothing.

NAIL TRIMMING

Back in the beginning, as part of the socializing process, you taught your tame bird to be comfortable with having his feet handled. Have you ever played "This Little Piggy Went to Market" with him? Stroke his feet, pick them up one at a time and tell him how beautiful and strong they are. Lay him on his back in your lap and let him grasp your fingers with his feet and play with them. Have an emery board or heavy duty fingernail file handy and let him see it and get used to it. Let him watch you using the file on your own fingernails. While he is standing on the floor perch touch his feet with the file but do nothing else. When he seems to pay no more attention to it, briefly touch one nail with it. If he shows no reaction, you can P&R. Then try another nail or two, and again if your bird accepts it with no reaction, P&R. Do this over the course of several days.

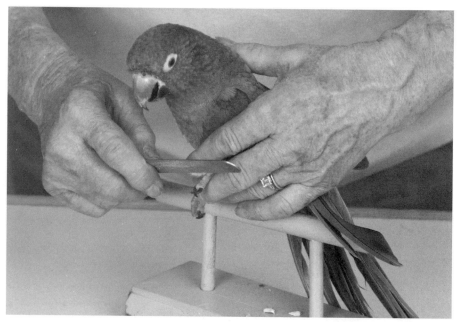

I'm getting a manicure and a pedicure. Does nail polish come next?

Take a Tip from a Pro Trainer

Here's a training suggestion from my friend and fellow bird trainer John Vincent: Some people find trimming a bird's nails with the bird inside his cage hanging on to the side of his cage provides a better view of the nail, reducing the risk that you could cut too much nail off.

One method of training a bird for this type of nail trimming would be to teach your bird to hang on the side of the cage with his nails sticking out for full access. With your bird in the enclosure, place your bird's favorite treat in the location you would like to do the nail trimming. When he climbs over to the side of the enclosure to get the treat, say "good" and give your bird the treat. Repeat this step several times until your bird readily moves to the nail trimming location for the treat. Next add a cue to the behavior. The cue could be placing your empty hand over the location, and after the bird moves to the location say "good" and give the treat. Your hand provides a target for the bird, which guides him to the location you want. Build a strong reinforcement history so the bird readily moves to the desired location on cue.

Next, with the bird in the correct location, touch the bird's nail and say "good," and then give the bird the treat. Repeat touching the bird's nail many times to desensitize the bird to having his nails touched. Each time increase by small increments the time you touch your bird's nail before saying "good" and providing the treat. Do not hold your bird's foot, making him feel trapped. You need to take the steps slowly so as not to frighten your bird. If your bird gets scared, you may have great trouble getting your bird's trust back. This can take anywhere from a few days to a few weeks depending on your bird's trust.

When your bird is very comfortable with you touching his foot for several seconds, you can introduce the clippers. At first only touch the clippers to the bird's nail; do not clip any nail the first several times. Get your bird comfortable with the clipper before taking your first clip. Slower is better than faster. Now the time has come for the first clip. Ask your bird to move to the nail clipping location. When your bird is in position, clip a very small amount of nail, say "good," and give your bird a treat. Never take too much off your bird's nails, in case you hit the quick where nerves are located that cause him pain. In that case, he will understandably begin to refuse to move to the nail trimming location.

Next, pick one foot up and briefly touch the file to the bird's nails on the foot he is left standing on. When he tolerates this, you can try making a few filing attempts on that foot. You are slowly shaping him to accept his nails being filed so P&R each little step. I have found handing the bird a large nut that he has to hold in a foot to eat will often distract him from what I am trying to do.

Ignore him if he pulls his foot away and go back to a place where he was accepting your touch. Let him see that only standing quietly gets him a food reward. If you file his nails frequently, you should never have to use clippers. All you want to do is keep the tips blunted so they are not sharp when he is standing on your hand. If you cut his nails too short not only could they bleed, but he will also lose his ability to grip a perch firmly, which could cause him to fall. Using one of those special perches that they now sell for the bird market, which helps to keep the nails and beak blunted, can sometimes really help and may even eliminate your need to have to trim his nails. You'll know when your bird's nails need trimming as they'll appear overgrown or will be sharp on your skin when you pick him up.

If your bird likes to lie on his back in your lap, do the same thing—at first just touching his nails with the file. Give P&R when he lies quietly with no protest. Play with him that way each day, and slowly increase touching his nails and starting the filing process. If he is never hurt, he may just look at this new "thing" you are doing as just another "thing" he will accept for the P&R he gets.

As in all behaviors and tricks you can teach your pet, you can accomplish the same thing in many different ways. I try to give you at least one way that I am sure of and that has worked for me. But if it doesn't work for you, try other ways. Experiment to see what works best for you.

Julie Cardoza shows how her well-trained Red-fronted Macaw allows her wings to be stretched out.

WING TRIMMING

Whether to trim your bird's wings is a personal decision, and I am not going to get into the pros and cons of it here, as this is a book about teaching you how to train your bird behaviors and tricks. Many books, articles, and Web-sites are devoted to this subject, so I will leave it up to them to argue the benefits of clipping or not. As a trainer I can just say that most pet owners find clipped birds much easier to manage. You can always let your bird's wing feathers grow in again after basic train-ing if you wish. Here I am just going to tell you how to train your bird so he will allow you to clip his feathers, if that is your decision. I am not going to

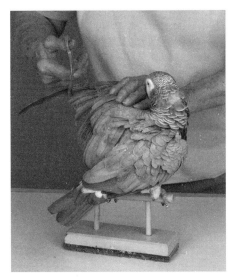

Having a trained bird makes wing clip-ping much easier.

even try to tell you what style of clip to use, or how much to clip from each wing (oh yes!, there are different styles and shapes for clipping wings and advocates for each one). I'll leave that to your avian veterinarian or other avian expert, but I will show you how to get your bird ready so he will accept the clipping with the least amount of trauma to you both.

As with the nail trimming described previously, make touching the bird's wings and extending them out a part of the initial socialization process. Touch your bird's wings from the very beginning of your relationship, pet them, stroke them, tell your bird how beautiful they are. With your bird standing on a T-stand, gen-tly grasp the bend of one wing and extend the tip of the wing outward only as far as he will let you. P&R each time he'll calmly let you do so. Shape him to allow you to extend the wing fully, and P&R each little step along the way. Do this first with one wing and then the other. Leave the scissors on the tabletop in full view so he will get used to seeing them. Make no attempt to use them at this time, but you can handle them to let him see they will not hurt him. Only after your bird is comfortable with your extending his wings fully should you pick up the scissors and just lightly touch his wings with them. Don't let him grab for them and don't try to cut a feather yet. Progress slowly. P&R each little improvement. Only after your bird is completely okay with you handling his wings and extending them, and only after you know exactly where you will cut, should you proceed to that first feather. Hopefully he will remain calm and allow you to clip. If not, go back to where he was accepting the procedure and start again from there. Progress lit-tle by little until he will calmly allow you to trim his wings.

GETTING INTO A CARRIER

Most companion birds are going to need to be transported somewhere in their lives in a carrier of some sort—whether to travel to a veterinarian, go to work with

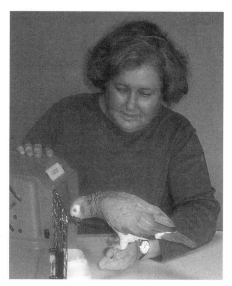

Diane Grindol easily puts Kiri into a carrier.

you daily, or transport in the event of a natural disaster or other emergency. Obtaining a carrier and preparing your bird to accept travel in it is very important. For flying with you, airlines will accept only the dog-type carriers that will fit under the seat in front of you, or the larger dog kennels that can travel in the baggage compartment. I prefer these types of carriers not only because they are sturdy, but because they allow the bird a certain amount of protection and privacy. The clear plexiglass ones might be esthetically pleasing to you, but they don't give the bird any feeling of protection from the scary things he might be seeing for the first time while traveling with you.

Whatever style of carrier you choose, do get your bird used to it before it is needed. Start training when your bird is slightly hungry; place yummy treats in the carrier for him to find. Let him think of the carrier as a neutral place to be and certainly not frightening. When you first enclose him in it, only pick it up and carry it a short distance, maybe just into the next room, where you can then give him lots of P&R. Definitely don't make his first trip in a carrier end up in a veterinary office if you can help it. Daily practice placing him in the carrier and taking him on progressively longer outings to fun places. Always tell him ahead of time where and how he will be going. Our parrots understand a lot more than we give them credit for.

TOWELING

Teaching a bird to accept being placed in a towel can be a very important husbandry procedure. Towels are not just for baths; they can be used to capture birds for being taken out of their cage, for restraining them for nail and wing clips when necessary, and for veterinary procedures. So it's a good idea to get your bird used to towels. If your bird has had no previous bad experience with towels, then teaching him about towels can be a lot easier. Start with making it a game. Place a regular hand-sized towel on the bed, let the bird walk on it and examine it if he wishes. Play a game of peek-a-boo with it, draping part of it over your bird as he will allow. Giggle and laugh with him as you play. If he likes cuddling, wrap him up in the towel and cuddle him in whatever way he is used to. After a bath you might wrap him up in the towel to help dry him off. In other words, make the towel a non-threatening object.

If your bird has already had a bad experience with becoming frightened by being toweled, try very slowly to get him to accept a towel without a lot of panic. Don't use a towel to restrain him as long as he is wary. Start with a washcloth and use lots of P&R until

Diane prepares to towel a bird.

he will at least tolerate one being used around him. Then work up to a hand towel and try the cuddling and playing routine described earlier. In the future, if someone needs to grab or restrain your bird, working on this husbandry behavior should make it a lot easier for a person having to restrain your bird and for your bird.

My avian veterinarian, Dr. James Onorati of Des Moines, Washington, uses this method when toweling a bird who is friendly: He holds the bird on his right hand and secures the foot of the bird with his right thumb. Then he tucks one end of the towel under his chin and holds the other end out to his left with his left hand. He then brings the bird on his right hand in close to his chest in front of the towel and wraps the bird up with the other end of the towel in his left hand. He quickly has the bird wrapped and secure, and amazingly this method doesn't seem to unduly alarm the bird.

MOVING FROM PLACE TO PLACE

Our birds are built to fly speedily from one place to another. Many companion birds have clipped wings, however, and rely on humans for transportation around the house.

It's easiest when both you and your bird cooperate to move smoothly and accomplish this without a hassle. When your bird doesn't understand where you're

This Cockatiel displays considerable trust to be held this way.

going, he may jump off your arm, refuse to go in his cage, or head back the direction from which you were coming. This inevitably happens when you're late for work and need to get your bird and house secured before you leave!

A bird is immobilized when you hold your hand over his back, keeping his wings at his side. That sounds simple enough, but to a bird, this can be a very threatening action. Birds are prey animals, and their instincts tell them that they could become someone's lunch when they're restrained. With your reassurance, a bird can learn to be held in this way.

Work in small steps. Start by putting your hand near your bird's back and then withdraw it. When he is comfortable with that action, hold your hand over your bird's back, actually touching it briefly. Use a word or a phrase that will mean you're on the move with him. Perhaps "let's go" or "hang in there" will do. Next, start gently putting pressure on your bird with your hand when it is over his back and eventually progress to holding down his wings. Sometimes cuddling him to your chest at this time helps.

When your bird is comfortable with the action of using your hand to hold down his wings, take a few steps. This method of transportation will become second nature to you and your bird over time.

Of course, you two can move from place to place in other ways. You can gently take both your bird's legs and dance from place to place. He can climb on a stick at your command, and then stay there, and be whisked to his cage or a play stand. The important thing is to start talking to your bird while these actions are taking place. Use a word or a phrase consistently with these actions. That's how you communicate with your bird. It eliminates the surprise factor for him. When he knows what you want and what you are doing by your actions, he is less likely to feel that you are being unpredictable or even threatening. When he has words or actions he can recognize, his life is less frustrating.

Another way to safely transport your bird from one location to another is by holding onto his toes. If during the socializing and taming process you have touched and played with his feet, then touching them now as he sits perched on your hand should not be too big of a leap.

With your bird perched on your index finger, start moving your thumb over toward your bird's foot. In each successive practice with this maneuver, move your thumb closer until you touch your bird's foot briefly. P&R. Over time, exert some pressure and use your thumb to clamp your bird's front toes down securely to the top of your hand. If he's a parrot, he is zygodactyl, meaning he has two toes on each foot pointing forward and two toes on each foot pointing back. Holding his toes down with your thumb is a way you can carry your parrot from room to room without having him fly off your hand. It does require trust on the part of the parrot, who does not like being restricted. Work up to this action slowly. You'll find it very useful when you and your bird have mastered it.

Place your thumb gently but firmly over your bird's foot to keep him secured in place, as demonstrated with this Ducorps Cockatoo.

Chapter 5

Tricks That Don't Require Props

Now we are ready to start to train that first trick. Let's do a quick review. You have tamed your bird so you can handle him readily; he will step onto your hand; you can pick him up with your hands over his back; you can touch his feet and under his wings; and he will accept food from your hand. You are at least a number 5 in the Tameness Scale discussed in chapter 2, "Preparations for Training." You understand the training diet and how to manage your bird's food intake so he will be moderately hungry but not starved. You have selected a treat to be used as a reward for correct responses. You have prepared the training area complete with T-stand and training table. It is an area that is free from noise and distractions and away from the bird's own cage as well as other birds. You have taken the bird to the training area ahead of time to familiarize him with the surroundings. Now you are ready to start training your parrot.

If you can't do all this, please go back and review the previous two chapters as we are assuming at this point you have a tame, well-socialized bird. If your bird has other behavioral problems, mainly biting, try to resolve this issue before starting to trick train. You won't get far if you are constantly worried that your bird will bite you.

FIRST TRAINING LESSONS

Take your bird to the training table and place him on the T-stand. For large birds like cockatoos and macaws, a floor stand is easiest. They come in two heights; one is about waist height for those who want to sit, and there are taller ones for those who prefer to stand while they train. For smaller birds, which is just about everything else, use a tabletop T-stand. You can stand or sit at the training table, whichever is easiest for you. Height dominance, considering whether your bird is above or below your head, is not a factor in this kind of training. Either position is acceptable.

With the bird sitting comfortably on the T-stand or similar perch in front of you, feed him a treat and talk to him quietly. Using the *come* command, have the bird step onto your hand and then back to the perch with the *perch* command; see chapter 4, "Necessary Obedience Skills (Husbandry Behaviors)," for more on training both commands. Even though these are behaviors

Aztec, a Blue-headed Pionus, is comfortable and ready to train on his tabletop T-stand.

your bird already knows, do them a few times as a warm-up. Give your bird praise each time he performs them correctly and give him the special treat you have selected. Remember, you are going to feed your pet this treat only when you are training. To be really effective, do not give him this treat at any other time. My smaller birds love safflower seeds; the larger birds get small pieces of peanuts or walnuts. I will often refer to the treat in this book as a seed, but remember, it can be anything the bird seems to really enjoy.

Give your bird a treat, and as he takes the treat from your hand, praise him. I say "good," "good boy," "good job," or "good baby." It matters little what words you use; it's the tone of voice that is important. These are our praise words, or as some call them, *bridge* words. The praise word is sometimes referred to as a bridge because it not only tells the bird that he has performed whatever action you called for correctly, but that a treat and reward will be forthcoming. It is supposed to bridge the gap between the bird's behavior and the reward. In theory, when the bridge word is paired with the treat enough times it becomes synonymous with the treat, so the bird will work just for the word. I have not found this to be quite true. I find that offering a food reward is still the most reliable way to train. And, of course, there is really no "gap" between the praise and the reward after a bird has completed a trick. The bird is on the table right in front of me. The combination of praising and rewarding is done at the same time.

THE TURN AROUND

This is a simple first trick, and it might not interest you as a future trick, but what you are teaching the bird here is more than just a trick. You are teaching him how to learn, what is expected of him, and how he will be rewarded. Remember, a bird will only repeat a behavior for which he is compensated in some way.

The way I like best to teach this trick incorporates what will become the visual cue. Birds are much more responsive to visual cues than to verbal cues. Even though you may teach both the verbal and the visual cue at the same time, you will probably be dropping the verbal one eventually, especially if you ever have your bird perform for others. You can be talking, saying anything, and still have the bird respond to a visual cue that can be reduced to a bare minimum. The audience will think the bird is reading your mind! But for now, teach both. The verbal command makes the bird pay attention and gives the trainer focus.

Start with your bird on the table T-stand or on a floor perch. With this trick you can certainly use the target stick, as described in chapter 3, "Training Basics," to get the bird to turn first half way and then all the way around.

Hold a seed in your right hand at about the bird's eye level; let the bird see the seed. Tell him "turn around." I usually start with having the bird turn to his left to face back, but it really doesn't matter which way you want the bird to turn as long as you are consistent. As the bird reaches for the seed, move your hand around the bird to his back so that the bird must first turn his head and next, his whole body, to follow and reach for the seed. Some birds will turn all the way around the first time, but if your bird turns only part way, P&R him at that halfway point. Then coax him to turn the rest of the way around by following the

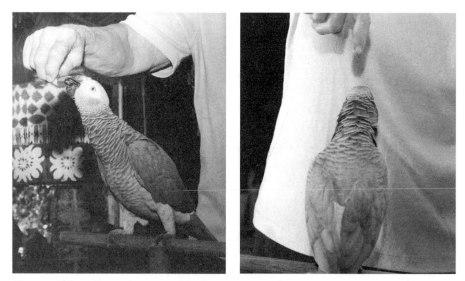

Kiri, an African Grey, demonstrates the turn around.

Turn Around Times Three

Sally Blanchard is a parrot behavioral consultant as well as the editor and publisher of the *Companion Parrot Quarterly*. I will always remember a show I did for Sally in Oakland, California. I was demonstrating the *turn around* and how to teach it when I noticed the audience laughing. I knew I wasn't that funny so I indicated by miming I wanted to know what was so funny. Some people in the audience pointed to my parrots who were behind me on their stands. Not only was the bird I was demonstrating with on the table turning around, but the other birds behind me on their stands were also turning around on my cues and signals. Now those were well-trained birds!

seed in your right hand. What we are doing is "shaping" his behavior by talking just little steps toward the final goal. Use the simple command "turn around" each time you ask him to turn. After the bird turns from front to back and then back to front readily, insist he turn all the way around before he gets his reward.

In the next step, let the bird follow the seed around in your right hand but hold another seed in your left hand. When the bird has completed the turn, reward him with the seed from your left hand. Gradually raise your right hand a little higher each time the trick is successfully repeated.

After he's followed the food all the way around a few times, turn the motion your right hand makes into a hand signal without the food. Give the reward from your left hand with each success. Have the right hand just make a small circle above the bird's head, being sure to immediately reward the correct behavior with a seed from the left hand. Eventually you will be able to just circle the right index finger above the bird, and if you wish, drop the command altogether. For now be satisfied with the bird just turning around on the T-stand, even if he does so a bit awkwardly or slowly.

Think of what your pet has learned in just a few minutes. He has heard a command *(turn around)*, he has seen and learned to respond to a visual cue (the right hand, index finger circling over his head), he has learned that the word "good" means his owner is pleased, and finally, that he will get a special treat. And all he had to do was turn around!

When your bird has grasped the idea for the *turn around,* move on to another trick. Don't bore the bird with endless repetition. Keep this and all future lessons exciting. Be excited yourself by each small increment of success your bird achieves and let him know it.

When your bird completely understands that a small circle of the index finger means he is to turn around, have him try the *turn around* just on the training table, and not on a perch. When he will turn readily, make the visual cue smaller each time. Eventually, you can casually use it to signal your bird to do a 360-degree turn while taking the ball to the basket. Or use it to have your bird spin around while lifting a barbell. Or have your bird pirouette or dance to music.

Your bird may surprise you if after learning the *turn around* by turning to his left as he turns to face back, he all of a sudden turns around to his right instead (when you give the signal). He has just expressed his preference for turning the other way. That is fine! Teaching him to go either way will make an even cuter trick. You could narrate his behaviors, as though he can't make up his mind, he turns this way and then that. The showmanship comes later. You don't have to hurry things.

THE WAVE

Teach your bird to *wave* with the left foot and *shake hands* with the right. Don't let your bird do both these behaviors with the same foot, since it will only lead to confusion later. Most birds are left-footed (oh yes, birds have definite foot preferences) and will step onto a perch with the preferred foot first. If your bird is left-footed, teach the *wave* first because it is easier. If you have a right-footed bird, you might want to reverse it and teach the *shake hands* trick first. Directions for that trick are covered in the next section.

To teach the *wave,* have your bird sitting on the T-stand. Wiggle the fingers of your right hand as in a small wave as though you were waving goodbye. Say "wave," or whatever verbal cue you wish. It could be "hello," "good bye," "salute," or some other appropriate word or phrase. It really makes no difference as you can drop the verbal cue and just go to the visual cue soon. After your bird has mastered this trick, you will be asking him to wave goodbye or even say hello with just the small wave of your fingers.

Cowboy, a Double Yellow-headed Amazon, demonstrates the wave.

To begin, wiggle your fingertips in front of him as in a small wave and then immediately proffer your left hand/finger for the bird to step onto. The bird will undoubtedly try to step forward onto your hand as in a step up. Do not let him! The minute you see him start to lift his left foot, pull your hand away, P&R with the reward you

Innovative Behaviors

Be on the lookout for any creative behavior your bird does. In trick train-ing, these are called innovative behaviors. For example, I was teach-ing the wave in the usual manner to RIki, a Lilac-crowned Amazon, when he decided to scratch his head with his left foot. I guess he felt as long as he was lifting it anyway, he might as well make use of it. I quickly P&R'd him. I wasn't sure what I would do with this behavior at the time, but thought it might be useful. He then did it on his own again. I praised and rewarded him each time I saw him do it. He decided that was what I must have wanted. When I gave him the cue to wave, his foot came up and did the quick scratching movement, although he wasn't actually scratching himself. That became one of the most original waves I have seen. He would lift his foot and quickly move it up and down several times, like scratching in mid-air. I think he liked doing it!

Riki, a Lilac-crowned Amazon, doing his special wave.

are holding in your right hand. It won't take very many repetitions before he gets the idea that all he has to do to get the reward is to lift his left foot. You no longer need to offer him your hand for him to step on, just wave your fingers and your bird will begin tentatively raising his foot. When he does this readily, start with-holding the seed just a few seconds longer. The usual reaction is to lift the foot a little higher. When the bird gets the foot as high as you think he is going to and then starts to drop it, reward him immediately, and you have the beginning of the wave motion. Do this only until the bird is lifting his foot readily, and you can delightedly praise him. That is enough for his first lesson on this trick. Move on to another trick. Keep training sessions fun and interesting for your bird.

Teaching these first two tricks should have taken about half an hour. If you are still having fun, and the bird is still interested and watching you fully, move on to trick three. This is not too much to teach in one session, and you will see that your bird actually seems to enjoy it. Don't worry about your bird doing a trick perfectly. All you want your bird to do now is to get the idea. Perfection can come later.

The wave becomes a salute.

SHAKE HANDS

Shake hands is an easy trick to teach after you have successfully taught your bird the *turn around* and the *wave*. In fact you will find that each succeeding trick you teach becomes easier now that your bird has learned how to learn and how to please you. With your bird on the T-stand as before, offer your *right* hand this time, across his body to in front of his right foot. Remember, the *wave* is done with the *left* foot, *shake hands* with the *right* foot. An easy way to remember this is that when we shake hands with someone, it is usually with our right hand. You want to make it easy for another person to shake hands with your bird when they are invited to do so.

In the beginning, your bird will undoubtedly try to step onto your hand with his left foot as that is what you wanted before. Don't let him. Insist he raise his right foot and try to step onto your hand with that foot. Be persistent and eventually he will try. Then follow with lots of praise and the reward. Don't let him transfer any weight to your hand, just let him touch your hand with his right foot.

It will amaze you how quickly your bird will get the idea after having gone through the other two tricks. He has learned that all he has to do is something simple like raise a foot, and he gets fussed over and a treat. Birds are very smart and after you show them what you want them to do, they are usually more than happy to comply. Wait until the next lesson, and only after your bird has placed his foot on your proffered finger fairly readily, should you attempt to raise and lower your hand as in the traditional *shake* motion. Finally, lightly touch the top of his foot with your thumb. If you have done all the taming preparation mentioned earlier, then touching your bird's feet will not alarm him. You are preparing him for the time someone might just grab his foot and try to shake it more vigorously.

In a future session, when the bird really indicates he understands shaking hands, you can make this trick more interesting by having someone else who your bird knows and likes, come to the

Kiri is being taught to shake hands with another person.

training area and shake hands with your bird. You will, of course, instruct the new person how to hold her hand out to the bird and how to let the bird just put his

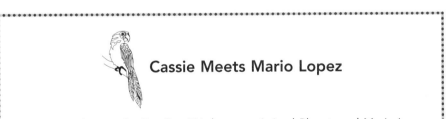

Cassie Meets Mario Lopez

I was appearing on the *Pet Star* TV show, on Animal Planet, and Mario Lopez was the host. He traditionally goes backstage before each contestant is introduced and meets that person and their pet. He greeted me and asked whether my bird was friendly and whether he could hold her. He has been bitten by several of the supposed *pets* brought to the show so he says he is always careful to ask before trying to pet or touch an animal. I said yes, of course, he could hold my bird (it was Cassie, my Black-headed Caique) and that my bird would also like to shake hands with him. I then showed him how to just gently offer his hand and let Cassie place her foot on it. He wasn't to grab for her foot.

All was fine and Mario went on stage to announce me. I walked out holding Cassie on my left hand. We chatted for a minute and then he said, "I understand your dog will shake hands with me." I hesitated, then said, "Well, she will, but Cassie is a bird, not a dog." He said "Oops. Stop everything. Let's do that over." I was sent back out, and we had to repeat the sequence. Cassie did fine, she shook hands with Mario, went on to do her series of tricks, and then Mario took her again and wanted to hold her the rest of the time I was on stage. I had to reach over and take her from him when it was time for me to leave. Everything turned out fine. We won that *Pet Star* segment and a $2,500 prize. See what it's possible to do by training your bird?

foot on her hand. When he does and you both fuss over him and feed him, you are on your way to teaching your bird to perform in front of others. There is nothing worse than telling your friends how smart your bird is and then not being able to show off for them because when they come over to see him, the bird won't do a thing. Teach your prize pupil the fun of performing for others in little ways right from the beginning.

The final step for the *shake hands* trick is to take your bird away from the training area and have him shake hands first with someone he knows and finally with a stranger.

REVIEW OF FIRST TRAINING SESSION

At the end of your first session training with your bird, you might want to review the three behaviors you have just taught. If, however, either of you are tired, then stop the session. Finish the lesson with something he did well. Praise him, reward him, and return him to his cage. Give him more treats and praise him there so he won't think he is being punished by being taken back to his cage. Then leave him. Don't follow with a play session. Let the training sessions become his special time with you, and your bird will look forward to them.

This first session should have taken thirty to forty-five minutes, longer if you were both having fun, shorter if either you or the bird got stressed. Help the bird to have as many successes as possible. Reward each little increment along the way. It is much better to guide him to the right response than to have to correct the bird for a wrong one. If the bird does not do something right, ignore it and try it again another way so that your bird can be rewarded for making a correct move. If your bird doesn't understand something, it is your, the trainer's, fault, not the bird's.

HIGH FIVE

After you have taught the *wave* and your bird is steady with it, you might want to try the *high five*. Give the signal for the *wave* but when the bird's foot reaches as high as it can, reach out and lightly touch his foot with your open hand. Be in a jovial mood and make this a fun trick when you ask your bird to "gimme five." Always give your bird lots of praise and a reward for his effort. He will catch on quickly.

THE KISS

If you have a bird that is at all aggressive, or that you think might bite, then don't try this next trick. I am including it only because it has been requested. It is easy to teach and doesn't involve a prop. With your bird sitting on a T-stand, hold his favorite treat between your teeth and let him see it. Point with your hand (either one) to your mouth and say "kiss." Bring your face close to the bird so he can easily see the seed and reach up to take it from you. If your bird is gentle, you won't have to worry about being bitten. Birds seem to take things very carefully from the mouth. Do this about twice, letting him take the seed from your teeth.

Next, indicate that your bird should give you a *kiss* with the seed held in your teeth. But as he reaches for it, cover the seed with your lips and just let him touch your lips. Reward him with a seed from your other hand. Do this a few times. If he doesn't get the idea, let him see the seed held between your teeth again, but prevent him from taking it by closing your lips over it and reward him for just touching your lips with a seed from your hand. When he starts reaching up on his own and just touching your lips with his beak, you can stop holding a seed in your teeth. Just point to your lips and say "kiss" as you bring your face down to your bird. Your bird will probably learn this easily in one lesson, and most birds seem to like it.

Then go the next step, probably in the second lesson, with picking the bird up and bringing him to within kissing range of your mouth. Have him reach for you to give you a kiss, instead of you lowering your lips to him. He is supposed to be the kisser now. As a final step, when your bird gets really good and trustworthy about performing this behavior, have him kiss someone else.

I made the mistake when I first taught this trick of selecting my husband, Keith, to be the kissee. He knew and liked Cassie, my Black-headed Caique, so I didn't foresee any problems, but there was one. My husband has a beard, and my bird in no way wanted to kiss that. As I brought her up to my husband's face Cassie just leaned back as far as she could and made her concerns obvious. My husband likes my birds and will interact with them when necessary, but he is definitely not the huggy, kissy, cuddling type that I am, so I surmised that he had just never had his face that close to her before. But after a few treats and much encouragement Cassie decided it was okay to kiss him!

When a new kissee is presented to your bird (preferably someone he knows), be prepared to start from the beginning of the kiss sequence. Have the new kissee hold the treats in his

Kiri enjoys giving Keith a kiss.

teeth just like you did to start and work from there. It will probably take only one kissee for the bird to then generalize and figure out he is to kiss whomever you indicate. Generalizing is another great ability our parrots have that we will use again and again.

NOD HEAD YES

Start with your bird sitting on a T-stand. Hold a piece of food in your fingers and move it up and down, so that your bird follows the movement, and his head is nodding up and down. I move my hand from up to down and back up in a quick movement that has evolved into the signal for this trick. You will need to repeat this a number of times before your bird understands what you are asking him to do. Eventually he will understand. I find myself also nodding my head and saying "yes" as I teach this.

Some birds will bob their whole bodies up and down so this action could be made into another innovative trick for a whole body *yes*. My Caique moves her head in a quick series of up and down movements so I captured that with P&R to make it into her way of saying "yes."

Some birds might grab your finger and pump on it as a baby does begging for a feeding. Praise and reward it for another innovative way of saying "yes."

SHAKE HEAD NO

This is another easy trick to teach. There are at least four ways in which it can be taught. Try each and see what works best for you.

Method One

The slowest but most obvious way to train the *shake head no* is to hold a piece of food in your hand and move it back and forth in front of the bird's face. Get him to follow the motion with his head, approximating the side to side shake of a "no" motion. I find that a bird learns slowly from this method and requires many repeats, so I don't use it very much. I did acquire my visual cue from this method, however. The visual cue I use is holding my thumb over my forefinger in front of the bird as though holding a seed. Over time, I can give the signal from farther and farther away. You can use any signal you want, like wagging your finger in the familiar *no-no* manner. I would not use the verbal cue of "no" with this trick for obvious reasons.

Method Two

The second method of teaching this trick is to gently blow in your bird's face. Most birds will immediately shake their heads when you blow on them. Couple this with your signal enough times, P&R him each time he shakes his head, and you soon have an approximation of a "no."

Method Three

The third method, if you have a bird who will absolutely not shake his head when you blow gently on him, is to place a small piece of clear tape on the back of his neck feathers. The bird, since he cannot reach it with his beak, will shake his head vigorously to try to get it off. Your P&R will stop the action momentarily as the bird eats his treat, but soon he will be trying to shake it off again. Be alert, give your signal at once, and again P&R. It should only require a few repetitions for your bird to get the idea. Then take the tape off immediately!

Method Four

Of course, if you are lucky enough to have a bird who sways back and forth on occasion, first try to figure out what triggers him to do so. As I mentioned, an innovative trick is an action a bird does on his own that we capture with P&R and then develop a cue for, so that the trick can be repeated on command. (I will talk more about those tricks and how to teach them in chapter 10, "Innovative Tricks.") Swaying back and forth can be a very distinct behavior so when you see your bird doing that, quickly P&R. When you've repeated this often enough and capture it on cue, it can lead to a very interesting way for your bird to say "no."

TAKE A BOW

With your bird sitting on his T-stand, bring your two index fingers gently up and under his wings. This will cause your bird to lift his wings slightly. Praise and reward your bird. If you have done all the preliminary work outlined before starting to train, you will have included touching the bird under his wings so this movement of yours should not overly disturb your bird. (You will be at number 7 on the Tameness Scale discussed in chapter 2.)

With this trick, all you want your bird to do is slightly lift his wings and drop his head. Usually a bird will automatically lower his head as his wings are raised. I do use a verbal cue for this trick. I say, "Take a bow." I use the verbal cue strongly on this trick as the trick is usually performed with the bird facing the audience and away from me; thus, he cannot see a visual cue from me. This trick is usually done on a table perch after completing another trick, or at the end of a performance. If your bird is to be on your hand or arm when he performs the *bow,* where he can see you, you can use the visual signal of two fingers held in a V shape. After training your bird to lift his wings slightly using the index fingers of both hands, it is easy to switch to the one hand V signal.

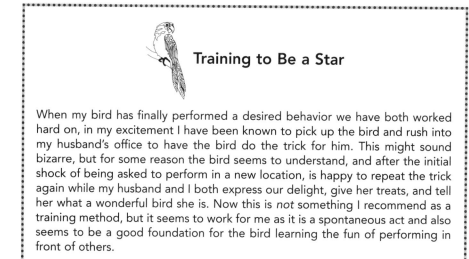

Training to Be a Star

When my bird has finally performed a desired behavior we have both worked hard on, in my excitement I have been known to pick up the bird and rush into my husband's office to have the bird do the trick for him. This might sound bizarre, but for some reason the bird seems to understand, and after the initial shock of being asked to perform in a new location, is happy to repeat the trick again while my husband and I both express our delight, give her treats, and tell her what a wonderful bird she is. Now this is *not* something I recommend as a training method, but it seems to work for me as it is a spontaneous act and also seems to be a good foundation for the bird learning the fun of performing in front of others.

BIG EAGLE

I make this trick different than the *take a bow* as it is used differently. With the *big eagle* I want the bird's wings fully opened and stretched out and his head up. As you remember, in the *bow* I only asked the bird to lift his wings slightly and to put his head down. You can give your bird a physical assist when training the *big eagle.* Standing in front of your bird while he is perched on his T-stand, say "eagle" and place your hands under his wings. Gently lift his wings as far as he will let you. P&R your bird. Repeat, showing your bird he is not being hurt, and he gets a treat each time he lifts his wings. Try to get your bird to lift his wings a little higher each time. Give him a chance each time you say "eagle" to lift his wings on his own. When you see him complying even a little to lift his wings by himself, P&R enthusiastically. From then on insist he make the effort on his own, and then only P&R when he lifts his wings higher. Don't be satisfied until he stretches his wings out completely. You can make your verbal cue the word "eagle." You can say, "What kind of a bird are you? Oh, you're an eagle!"

Another method that sometimes works to teach this behavior is to start with the bird on your arm or hand and then suddenly drop your arm slightly, or wiggle it to throw your bird off balance. Your bird will automatically open his wings to regain his balance and when he does you can capture the action and P&R.

Charlie, a Blue and Gold Macaw, does a big eagle.

Another signal you can use after the bird is readily lifting his wings for you, especially for a larger bird, is to have the bird on your arm, and then as you say the cue words, "What kind of a bird are you?" lift the bird over your head. As the bird lifts his wings, say, "Oh, you're an eagle!" as you proudly show him off. Lifting the bird overhead coupled with the cue words become the cues necessary for the action.

FLAP WINGS

For this trick all you want your bird to do is flap his wings on cue. I use it at the end of my show when I have the two smaller birds come forward on the table and take their "bows" to the audience. While they are doing that I hold my African Grey up overhead, and she flaps her wings heartily as I tell her to say goodbye to everybody.

Kiri flaps her wings at the thumb-on-foot cue.

Teaching this behavior is easy. Hold your bird on your hand and rock your hand just enough to make him flap his wings to regain balance and then P&R that behavior. To distinguish the cue for *flapping the wings* from the cue for *big eagle,* put your thumb on your bird's feet as you lift him up. Soon, the minute he feels your thumb on his feet he will start flapping. Easy, isn't it?

Chapter 6

Teaching the Basic Retrieve Command

The *retrieve* is probably the most important single behavior you can teach. It is the basis of up to 70 percent of all future tricks you will want to teach your parrot. Examples of tricks that are based on retrieve include *basketball, ring on the peg, coins in a bank,* putting shapes in the *puzzle board, stacking cups, turning a crank, pushing and pulling objects,* and much more (see chapter 7, "Simple Tricks Based on the Retrieve," and chapter 8, "Advanced Tricks Based on the Retrieve"). Since the *retrieve* is so important, take time and teach the concept thoroughly; don't try to rush ahead and teach each trick separately. Teaching the concept of having your bird bring any object to you that you indicate can make all future tricks much quicker and easier to teach, when the *retrieve* is taught properly.

Before you begin make sure that you have mastered at least the three basic beginning tricks of the *turn around,* the *wave,* and the *shake hands* (see chapter 5, "Tricks That Don't Require Props"). In those you were teaching your bird how to learn, what your praise word was, and that a reward would follow his best behavior. He should know these before you start the more difficult task of teaching the *retrieve.*

FIRST RETRIEVE LESSONS

Let's start with the basic idea of the bird picking up a designated object and bringing it to you. Start off with a simple object like a white plastic ring, plastic scoop, bottle cap, or plastic block. The object should be easy for your bird to pick up and appropriate to the size of your bird. Your bird should not be allowed to play with or chew on any of the props used in training, so don't tempt your bird with

These are examples of items that can be used for teaching the retrieve.

wooden objects. It is too easy for your bird to take a quick bite out of something wooden. Remember, everything is positive reinforcement at this stage so you don't want to have to take an object away from your bird, say "no," or show distress if he chews on a prop. Use plastic objects to start with. For the same reason, do not use one of the bird's toys as a *retrieve* object. This is serious training and you want your bird to take it seriously.

Place the chosen object to be retrieved on the training table. Place a seed, or whatever food reward you have decided upon, next to the object. Let your bird see you do it. Your bird will usually go directly to get the seed. Praise him and repeat, this time placing the seed on a different side of the object so the bird will have to look for it.

When your bird is comfortable getting the seed and is starting to expect it, hide the seed under the object. Your bird will now have to move the object to find it. You will only need to do each step a few times. Your bird will catch on quickly.

BRING IT TO ME

The verbal cue for this behavior is the string of words "bring it to me." I like this long verbal command because it has a different sound and is probably not something you have said to your bird before. Your bird will now associate these words with bringing you something and will forever after look for something to bring you when he hears the command. The visual cue is the hand held flat on the table, palm up. I am right-handed, so I use my right hand for this and have the treat ready to give my bird in my left hand. If you are left-handed, reverse the cue. This is one of the times you will be teaching a command and a signal together. You will probably always use these two together. This is an exception to the rule that you will usually need to use only one cue, either visual or verbal, to signal a behavior. Generally, it is the visual cue that becomes the predominant one. Birds, as you know, are very visually oriented.

Next, instead of putting the seed under the object, place your hand flat on the table, palm up as before, and tell your bird to "bring it to me." The bird will go to the object and look for the seed. When he doesn't find it, he will probably try to move the object looking for it. Immediately praise your bird and give him a seed from your other hand. Do this again, waiting just a few seconds longer to reward your bird. Usually in frustration the bird will try to pick up the object. Immediately praise and reward (P&R).

As soon as your bird picks up the object, try to slip your flat hand under the object so that it falls into your hand. This is the reason for this particular visual cue so that your bird will always associate your flat hand, palm up, with bringing you something. Your bird will soon get the idea that somehow the reward is now linked to picking up the object and then letting it fall into your outstretched hand. Slowly start withdrawing your hand so that it isn't directly under the object. Your bird will find that he has to stretch his neck a bit to get the object into your hand. Remember to profusely praise your bird for each little improvement. Soon you will have your hand far enough away so that your bird will have to take a step, holding the object, to place it in your hand. Move your hand a little farther away after each successful retrieve. Eventually your bird will have to walk to bring the object to you. Use lots of praise and rewards now when he does so.

Only use this first object long enough to see that the bird has the idea of bringing it to you and then change objects. Do not use a ball or anything that is round at this time. It is too easy for a ball to hit just part of your hand and be deflected so that you have to break your position and try to grab it. This spoils the point of the exercise. Save the balls for later when your bird is performing solidly in the *retrieve*. Select another object. You might have to start from the beginning with this object, too, but you will see your bird will catch on much more quickly and will soon be bringing that object to your hand. Then switch again. Keep changing the object to retrieve, making it a game so you keep your training interesting. Soon your bird should not hesitate to bring you whatever object you have put on the table.

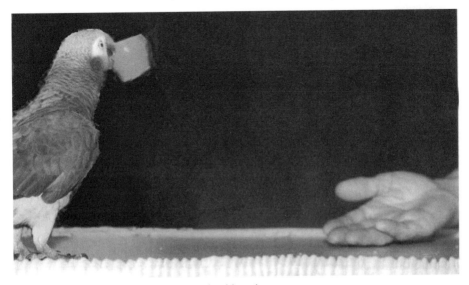

Kiri carries the object to an outstretched hand.

PLANNING AHEAD FOR OTHER TRICKS

Now you can advance to a finished trick. Do you want your bird to put a ball in a basket, maybe coins in a piggy bank, or play the shell game of finding a seed under a cup? How about teaching your bird a few basic colors while he is learning to put a ring on a peg? Stacking cups is easy to teach, and the cups are an easy-to-find prop. Think about it in advance and gather these objects for your bird to use while practicing the *retrieve*. Use different sizes and colored rings, various coins, cups, puzzle shapes, and if your bird has become a reliable retriever, you can add balls at this time. Make it fun for him to see whether he can bring you whatever you place out there. Use many different types of objects and have your bird bring them to you. Remember to praise and reward the bird after each successful *retrieve*. Don't forget to introduce the small white plastic rings usually found in sewing or craft stores that can be attached to the ends of strings for pull toys, bells, signs, and so on. They come in very handy for future tricks.

MOVING THE OBJECT AROUND

When your bird has become quite familiar with bringing you a variety of objects that you plan to use later as props, you can start teaching the concept of bringing the object to wherever you indicate, not just bringing the object to your hand.

First have your bird bring an object to your hand. Next move your hand to different places on the table so your bird learns to bring the object to wherever your hand is, not just when it is in front of your body. Make sure that one of the

Your hand indicates the box as the receptacle for the retrieved object.

positions is directly away from you so your bird can learn how to work away from you and toward an audience.

Next place the object in a container just large enough to hold the object. Have your bird take it out of the container to bring it to you. Move the container with the object to different places on the table. Finally place the object on the table and take the container yourself. Now you are going to ask your bird to bring you the object and place it in the container instead of in your hand. Do you see how you are progressing by just little steps for your bird to bring you anything you indicate and also place it anywhere you indicate?

Have your bird bring the object to you, but this time have your hand over the container and tipped toward the container so the object will fall into it. Remember to P&R after each successful *retrieve*. After a few times just indicate by tapping the container where you want your bird to place the object. You could use the target stick to lure the bird to the container, but I prefer to use my hand. Move the container to different places on the table so the bird learns to bring the object to wherever you indicate. Change objects frequently so your bird learns to bring you whatever to wherever. You are now ready to train that first trick based on the *retrieve*.

CARD TRICKS

Now that your bird has learned the *retrieve*, here are a few special card tricks that would be easy for him to learn. The following two tricks were designed by my good friend, Stan Kramien, a wonderful animal and bird trainer and also a very accomplished magician.

Cherchez La Femme

Stan says: "Here is a card trick that has worked well for me over the years. Showmanship is always the word, don't take the act too seriously, your audience will have fun if you are having fun. Believe me, it shows.

"This trick is based on the old three card monte, or *cherchez la femme* (find the lady). It is a betting game and is still played on the streets of New York. You will need one simple prop, a rack for the cards to stand in. You can make one. Use a 1 × 1 about 10 inches long

Stan Kramien.

if you are going to use regular-size playing cards. I prefer using the 4-inch jumbo cards as the audience can see them better. The jumbo cards can be found at local magic stores. If you are using them, then use a longer base at least 13 inches long. Saw a slit, as wide as the cards are thick, along the middle of the base, and deep enough to allow the cards to stand upright.

"Have this on the table along with three cards, two of which will be marked. Pick up the cards and show the audience a queen and two other cards. Place them in the rack with the faces toward the audience, backs toward you and your bird. Mix up the cards on the rack making sure the dot on the marked queen card is in the up position, and the other marked card with its dot is now in the down position, hidden by the rack. Move them around a bit, or better yet have the audience tell you where to place the cards. Tell them to just point as the bird can hear them if they call out.

"Put the bird on the table and ask him to pick out the queen card, from the back. Of course he easily does so. Send the bird back to his perch and mix the cards up again. Say, 'Does anyone want to bet?' Once again the bird picks the queen.

"Now explain to the audience that sometimes the bird wants them to win. Replace the cards, but this time switch the cards and place the queen card dot down, and the other card with a spot now in the up position. This time the bird picks the wrong card; the audience wins; and everybody is happy. Use a little imagination and play it up as a con game with the bird in control."

To teach this, put a card face down on the table. Place a big black dot on the back, near the top of the card. Ask your bird to "bring it to me," using *retrieve* cues. When your bird understands to bring you the marked card, then add another unmarked card. Keep insisting your bird bring you only the marked card. Keep changing the card's placement.

Next, put the cards in the rack with their backs facing you and your bird. The marked card, the queen, will have a dot at the top of the card. Ask your bird to "bring it to me" and allow your bird to select only the marked card. Continually change the card placement. When your bird is selecting the marked card reliably, start using cards with a smaller dot. As the bird understands he is to bring you only the marked card, make the dot as small as you think your bird will be able to see. The dot must be near the top of the card for the bird to see when it is placed in the up position and be covered by the rack when it is turned the other way around in the down position. Now he is ready to do the complete trick.

Find the Card

Here is another goodie from Stan: "Go to your local magic shop and buy a 'forc- ing deck' (all the cards are the same). Shuffle the cards and have someone in the audience pick a card. Have him show everyone in the audience what it is and then replace it in the deck. Shuffle the cards; then fan them out in front of the bird, backs of course to the audience. Have your bird take a card, and guess what, it is the same card! With a bit of showmanship, this can be a lot of fun. If you want a big laugh, when the audience is applauding, say, 'It's not that great a trick,' and turn the deck over in your hands and without saying anything, fan the deck out showing all the cards are the same."

Is This Your Card?

In this trick, which is one that I enjoy doing, you take advantage of your bird's natural inclination to bite things. Hold some cards up and allow him to take one. Encourage him to mouth it a little, and then P&R. When he will take a card, bite down on it a little, and then release it to you, you can proceed with this trick. Ask your bird to take a card. Show it to the audience without you looking at it and then replace the card in the deck. Next fan the cards and select the "mouthed, bitten" card and ask your bird whether that is his card. Cue him to shake his head no. Or you can approach the trick another way and select the wrong cards first and have him shake his head no; then you finally pick the "right" card, and he will nod his head yes, that you have finally picked the right card.

Pick a Card

Teach your bird to pick a marked card as taught previously, going from a large dot to a smaller one that can just barely be seen. For this trick, start by holding the marked card in your hand and let your bird take it from you that way, rather than from the table top as in previous tricks. When he takes the card readily and gives it back to you, add a second unmarked card so he now has to choose between the two cards and must pick the marked card. Keep changing the placement of the cards so first the marked card is on the left and the next time maybe on the right. When he reliably picks the marked card, add a third card. When he will again always pick the marked card, start decreasing the size of the mark so that the mark is just a small dot on the back of the card.

To do this trick you need an accomplice who knows the trick. Fan a deck out in front of the secret accomplice and have her pick a card; of course, she will pick the marked card. Have her show the audience the card and then replace it in the deck. Don't use a full deck on this one as it is just too many cards and makes it more difficult than necessary. Use approximately ten to fifteen cards. Shuffle the cards any way you want and then ask your bird to find the card the accomplice picked. Fan the cards, showing only the backs of the cards to your bird. Of course, your bird will also pick the marked card, which you can then proudly show the audience, to their amazement. What a smart bird you have!

Chapter  7

Simple Tricks Based
on the Retrieve

All of the tricks in this chapter are based on a thorough understanding of the *retrieve,* as taught in chapter 6, "Teaching the Basic Retrieve Command." Do not attempt to teach these tricks until your bird understands the *retrieve* concept completely.

Tricks using props will now be introduced. Instructions for making some of the simpler props are given in chapter 13, "Making Props," as well as ideas on where they might be purchased. Take time to introduce each prop to your bird before you start to teach the trick. As with new toys, some birds can be skittish around new props; others take them in stride. Introduce the new prop the same way you would introduce a new toy. Leave the new prop outside your bird's cage where he can see it for a few days. Just remember props are never to be treated as real toys and should never be placed inside the bird's cage or even left alone unsupervised with the bird. Never let your bird chew on or bite a prop. If you treat the prop carefully and with respect, the bird is apt to follow your lead. Handle the prop in your bird's presence to show him it is not dangerous. If the prop moves, show your bird this.

One way I use to introduce new props is to place the prop in the middle of the kitchen table and then my husband and I eat our meal around it. My birds come to the table and eat with us. They are allowed to approach a new prop centerpiece and touch and examine it if they wish. My husband and I just ignore it and eat our dinner as usual. The prop becomes like anything else I might put in the center of the table, like a new vase of flowers or a real centerpiece! My birds see us paying no attention to it and soon decide it is just another thing on the table with which they don't have be concerned.

My birds become accustomed to props by seeing that I don't react to them when they're included in daily activities. Here a basketball hoop on the far left is casually included in a shared lunch.

When your bird no longer shows fear or even real interest in a prop, you can then use the prop safely in teaching a new trick. A fear of new props will only last so long. After your bird has been introduced to many props and tricks, he will start to accept a new prop with a ho-hum attitude: "I wonder what Mom has for me now?"

BASKETBALL

Description: To perform this trick, the bird picks up a basketball from any location on the training table and drops it into the hoop.

Prerequisite: Your bird needs to know how to *retrieve,* as explained in chapter 6.

Equipment: For your basketball, especially at first, use a light wiffle ball. They have lots of holes in them and are light and easy for your bird to pick up. They come in many sizes and can be found in almost all pet stores. You will probably be able to find a basketball hoop. If not, you can use a plastic or even a paper cup, or whatever round container your ball will fit into easily.

Start training basketball by holding the basket at table height and gradually raise it. Poopsie, a Green-cheeked Conure, demonstrates.

Instructions: To start training your bird to put a basketball into a basket, first have your bird bring you a ball and place it exactly in your hand. This is the *retrieve* behavior you learned in chapter 6.

Next, have your bird bring you the ball and then indicate for him to place it in the basket, cup, or whatever you are using as a receptacle. This should be easy if you have followed all the training steps on the *retrieve*. You can tap the basket with a target stick or the back of your hand so that when your bird brings the ball to your hand it will fall into the basket. Do this a few times with the basket at table height and have your bird place the ball in the basket.

Gradually raise the basket higher until your bird really has to reach to put the ball in the basket. Use a close-ended basket so the bird can see that the ball is in the basket. If the basket is open-ended the ball will just fall out, and it will take longer for the bird to understand what he has achieved. To make this trick really impressive, make sure your bird has to reach high to put the ball in the basket. A low basket makes it look like your bird is just dropping the ball in and not really doing anything special.

After your bird has learned the *basketball* trick, he generally needs no visual or verbal cues. Place the ball on the table near the basket, and your bird should immediately pick up the ball and drop it in the basket after he has formed this association. Next, start placing the ball farther and farther away from the hoop,

On the Court

You can make the basic *basketball* trick different and interesting in numerous ways. Cassie, my Black-headed Caique, does her characteristic hops to the basket carrying the ball in her beak. Squawk, my Blue-crowned Conure, "dribbles" the ball, picking it up and touching it down several times as she moves down the court. Poopsie, my little Green-cheeked Conure, has to climb a ladder to reach the basket. Xena, my Hawkhead, does 360s (*turn arounds,* described in chapter 5, "Tricks That Don't Require Props") on her way to the basket. Another bird flies to the top of the basket, carrying the ball, and then drops the ball in from above. These are all advanced ideas. Wait until your bird is really comfortable with performing the basic trick before you start introducing variations.

Poopsie has to climb a ladder to reach the basket, a variation of the basketball trick.

until your bird will triumphantly carry it the length of the table to dunk it into the basket, to your delighted praise. Be sure to praise and reward (P&R) each little step and accomplishment along the way. Remember, only behaviors rewarded in some way will be repeated.

WASTEPAPER INTO A WASTEPAPER BASKET

Description: In this trick, the bird picks up wastepaper and places it into a wastepaper basket.

Prerequisite: The *basketball* trick, as described in the previous section.

Equipment: You will need a container to act as the wastepaper basket. A paper cup or similar receptacle will do nicely. Wad up some paper for the "trash."

Instructions: This is like a variation of the *basketball* trick. You ask your bird to bring you whatever you indicate and place it in the container you indicate, just as you did when you were teaching the *retrieve.* Ask your bird to bring you the wadded-up piece of paper, and then indicate for him to place it in the container/wastebasket. And you have another trick!

RECYCLING

Description: To perform this trick, the bird will pick up objects to be recycled and place them into appropriately marked containers such as paper, glass, and plastic. Like many people, your bird is probably concerned about preserving the environment. "Think globally, act locally" could be his motto.

Prerequisites: The previous trick, putting *wastepaper into a wastepaper basket.*

Equipment: I use three tin cans without their labels. I left one the natural tin color; the other two I spray painted orange and green, because those were the paint colors I just happened to have. Any colors will do other than the red, blue, and yellow you will be using for color identification tricks (see the *rings on the peg by color* section later in this chapter). I labeled the cans PAPER, GLASS, and PLASTIC on each side. This is for the benefit of an audience. You want them to be able to see what your bird is doing. A small bundle of newspaper pieces tied with a string could be used for one of the recycled objects. A small glass bottle or anything of glass of the appropriate size could be another object to recycle. For a third object any plastic item your bird can easily pick up will do.

Instructions: This trick is really a variation of the previous two tricks. This time, your bird will match objects and containers. After you have the setup, you teach your bird which object goes into which can.

Start with the paper, as it seems to be the easiest for a bird to pick up. Place the newspaper bundle and the can labeled PAPER on the training table. Have your bird bring the newspaper bundle to you and drop it into the can. These are all behaviors that your bird learned when you taught him to *retrieve,* so this should not be new to him. Put a second can on your training table next to the first one, but insist your bird continue to drop the newspaper bundle only into the one can. Let's say it is the silver can marked PAPER. You can even cover the top of the other can with your hand so that he has no choice in the beginning but to put the paper into the correct can. Make it easy for your bird to have as many successes as possible so you will have lots of chances to P&R. Keep the corrections to a minimum.

Keep switching the placement of the cans, so one time the silver can is on the left, the next time on the right. Use the name of the object you are asking your bird to pick up. You want your bird to learn the name for each recyclable. Say, "Bring me the *paper,*" putting emphasis on the word paper.

When your bird seems to have figured this out and will put the bundle of paper only in the can marked PAPER, move to another object, let's say the glass bottle. Do the same thing with that until your bird learns he is to put the bottle only in the can marked GLASS. Be sure to use the word "glass," to have your bird bring you the correct item each time you ask for it. Now use both objects and have the bird pick up only the one you ask for and place it into the correct can.

This is not an easy trick to teach, so take your time and put no pressure on your bird. Help your bird to have as many successes as possible by indicating the correct item or the correct recycling can. Don't let your bird depend on your indications, though, just offer a subtle help if he seems to need it. Sometimes all I have to say is "uhh," a soft deterrent sound, to make my bird stop and rethink where he is placing something. You don't need any strong words or sounds. Just be helpful when needed and then always give your bird lots of P&R when he does the trick correctly.

Only when your bird can place these two objects with reasonable accuracy should you add the third. Then go back to the beginning with the remaining plastic object and teach him to place it only in the remaining can marked PLASTIC. Finally, cautiously add the paper can and finally the glass can. To get accuracy is going to take time so take it slow and have lots of patience; your bird will understand in due time.

By using and emphasizing the name of the object constantly when teaching this trick, your bird will soon learn the name of each item and will eventually be able to respond by picking up only the object named and taking it to its correct container. In doing this trick, as with many of the others, don't have your bird always bring the objects to be recycled to cans placed in front of you. Teach your bird to work away from you as well with the cans toward the audience. It makes a much more pleasing presentation if your bird will pick up the requested object and take it to the cans that are on the audience's side.

RING ON THE PEG

Description: For this trick, the bird takes a ring and places it on a peg. The *ring on the peg* is an easy and fun trick to teach your bird.

Prerequisite: The *retrieve,* as learned in chapter 6.

Equipment: A base peg and a ring of matching color. The props are easy to make. The base peg part is just a flat square block, appropriate to the size of the bird, with a hole drilled in the center in which you fit a short dowel for the peg part. The peg prop will be described in more detail in chapter 13. It's the rings that are harder to find. Try to find different sizes of rings in the same color. Spray paint the base and the peg to match the ring color. The reason for all this is to make sure that your bird learns from the beginning to put a specific color ring only on a matching colored peg. This is the basis for your bird learning his colors, as described in the next trick.

Instructions: Begin by putting your colored ring on the table. Ask your bird to bring it to you just as he has done before when learning to *retrieve.* But this time

Hold the peg this way to help your bird learn how to put a ring on it. Xena, a Hawk-headed parrot, is learning this trick.

have the peg base under your hand with your palm up as in the "bring it to me" cue, with the peg sticking up through your fingers. When your bird brings the ring, you can help him to put it on the peg by spearing the ring with the peg as necessary. As the bird gets the idea, remove your hand so your bird sees the ring fall onto the peg base. This is always a fun trick to watch a bird learn. Sometimes a bird will flip the ring over his head and be so surprised. Sometimes he will carry it low and even stumble over it. Then he will hold it out in front of himself and hope it will land on the peg. Finally he will learn to touch the end of the peg with his beak and deftly slide the ring onto the peg. After your bird has the idea of how to do this trick, work with different sizes of rings. You will be surprised at how quickly your bird learns to handle all sizes of rings, from the largest to the smallest. Resist the temptation to use a variety of colors of rings. At this time use only one color of ring and a matching colored peg. You are preparing your bird for the next trick, when he will be asked to match rings and pegs of different colors.

RINGS ON THE PEG BY COLOR

Description: Now that your bird can put a ring on a peg, you're going to make the trick harder. In this trick the bird must pick up the color ring you ask for and place it on the matching colored peg. He must discriminate among differently colored rings and differently colored pegs, and he must follow your directions.

Prerequisite: The basic *ring on the peg* trick, as described previously.

Equipment: Rings and pegs of various colors. Three colors are plenty to begin with. Use the three primary colors of red, blue, and yellow if you can, as these make not only bright attractive props but are useful for teaching colors. Spray paint the bases and the pegs to match the ring colors.

Instructions: At first give your bird the blue ring to put on the blue peg with no other choices. Then add a red peg but insist he still put the blue ring on only the blue peg. Then add a yellow peg. Change the placement of the pegs so your bird doesn't think he should only put the ring on the peg in the middle spot, for instance. This would be learning the trick by position rather than color.

Next, switch to another colored ring, say the red ring, and work with only one peg, the red peg. Gradually add the second and finally the third peg for him to have to choose from. Repeat the process until he will readily put the red ring only on the red peg. Now go back to the blue ring and see whether he will still choose the blue peg for that ring. Don't be afraid to go back a few steps and repeat earlier training if he seems at all confused. Next add the red ring and ask your bird to place it on the red peg. Leave the two pegs, the red and the blue, out on the training table and have him alternate placing the rings on the two pegs. Be sure to change the placement of the pegs so he doesn't think the red ring always goes to the peg on the left side and the blue ring to the peg on the right side rather then placing them by color.

Matching the color ring with the same color peg teaches your bird color discrimination.

When your bird can place the two rings accurately, add the third ring and go through the same process. Start teaching the names of the colors now, telling your bird to put the yellow ring on the *yellow* peg. Emphasize the name of the color. You are now working on another level of color discrimination in which your bird will learn that certain colors have names.

When your bird seems to understand the connection between each ring and its similarly colored peg, place the rings in a pile on the table and ask him to put the rings on the pegs, letting him select a ring he wants and then put it on the matching colored peg. When he can do that readily you can go to the highest level where you tell him which ring he must pick up and put on the matching peg. To do this, go back a few steps and just ask your bird to bring you the red ring. He doesn't have to put it on a peg, just bring it to you.

Then work on having your bird bring you the blue ring and then the yellow one until he can bring you any ring from a grouping on the table when you ask for it by color. This task is more difficult and takes a bit of work and much repetition, but it is something you can keep working on as you teach other tricks.

Finally add the pegs and call out which color ring you want your bird to select. He must then put it on the matching color peg. The end result is quite spectacular and worth the extra effort. Teaching colors and their names can be the start of more advanced tricks where you ask your bird to bring you colored items when asked, just by naming the color.

RINGS ON THE PEG BY SIZE

Description: The bird selects the largest ring to place on the peg first and then places successively smaller rings, with the smallest one placed last.

Prerequisite: The basic *ring on the peg* trick, as taught previously.

Equipment: You'll need just one of the basic pegs and several rings of the same color that are different sizes.

Instructions: This is another fun trick to teach based on the *ring on the peg* trick. Teaching your bird to place rings on the peg according to size is a more difficult trick, so wait until your bird has learned many tricks before asking him to learn the size concept.

Start with two rings of the same color but one quite small and one quite a bit larger. Again, use a peg that is the same color as the rings so that your training is consistent with the *ring on the peg* trick you taught before. Ask your bird to place the largest ring on the peg first. Prevent him from taking the smaller ring by covering it with your hand or holding it down. Keep exchanging the places of the two different sizes of rings until your bird seems to grasp the idea of always picking up

Squawk puts rings on a peg in order of size, from the largest to the smallest ring.

the largest one. Do not have him put the smaller one on the peg at this point because you don't want him to think that the smaller ring is the treat getter. All you want him to do is pick the largest ring first.

Then add another size ring, somewhere in between the two sizes of rings you already have out on the training table. Again insist your bird always pick up the largest one first. Then ask him to get the next one, covering up the smallest one if he seems at all interested in it. Don't let him place it on the peg yet. He must always view that little ring as last. When he finally learns the difference between the two larger rings, then you can add the small ring and let him place it on the peg. Remember to keep rotating where you place the rings on the table so he doesn't inadvertently use placement to select the rings, instead of learning the concept of size you are trying to teach.

This trick is difficult to teach as you are working with a concept that is new to the bird and is more complicated than just placing a ring on a peg. Don't expect success overnight. Keep on teaching other tricks as you work on this one, to keep your bird's interest up and give him chances for lots of successes to praise with other behaviors.

RING ON YOUR FINGER

Description: Instead of putting a ring on a peg, in this trick the bird must take a ring and place it on your finger.

Prerequisite: The *ring on the peg* trick.

Accessories by Squawk.

Equipment: You need a large ring. Perhaps you can find a ring that resembles a piece of jewelry for this trick.

Instructions: You could use either your pinky finger, your index finger, or even your thumb. (I would not advise your middle finger, which could be misunderstood!) Just put your fist palm up on the table and extend whichever finger you choose. Tap this finger to indicate to your bird which finger to put the ring on. You can use a metal ring for this if you can find one that will slip on easily enough. Any ring will do, however, and it's a fun idea to play with.

LEI ON A DOLL

Description: Your bird puts a lei on a doll and ends with giving the doll a kiss!

Prerequisite: The *ring on the peg* trick.

Equipment: Select a doll that can stand upright on its own and that is appropriate in size to your bird. Then find or make a lei that will fit easily over the doll's head but yet stay on the doll's shoulders.

Instructions: Show your bird the doll with the lei around its neck. Then take the lei off the doll and give it to the bird and ask that he put it on the doll. Many birds understand immediately, but if not, you should put the lei on the doll and take if off several times to demonstrate.

Hey, a Kiss!

A kiss is always the lovely traditional way of ending the giving of a lei in Hawaii. For some reason my Black-headed Caique, Cassie, always wanted to bite the doll's face instead of just touching it with her beak. It wasn't worth trying to change her, so I would just ask her to place the lei on the doll and to give the doll a kiss. Then I would have to add, "Hey, I said a *kiss*, not a bite!" and let her do the trick her own way.

If your bird has done the *ring on the peg* trick enough times he will catch on to what you want here very quickly. To finish the trick, suggest that your bird give the doll a kiss. The *kiss* was taught in chapter 5.

STACKING CUPS

Description: The bird stacks cups in order of size from the largest cup to the smallest. This trick is one birds seem to learn easily and enjoy performing.

Prerequisite: The *retrieve*, as learned in chapter 6.

Will she get a kiss, too?

Equipment: You can find stacking cups sold as toys for infants in drugstores and toy stores. Use only every other cup in a set so the cups will nest easily inside each other and not be too tight.

Instructions: If you had your bird retrieve the cups when he was learning the basic *retrieve*, it should be easier for him to learn to stack them now.

Start by arranging the cups in order of size. Use only four cups at first. Place the second-largest cup in the center of the table and ask your bird to "bring it to me." Have the largest cup in front of you so when the bird brings the second-largest cup to you, you can indicate by tapping the largest one where you want the bird to put it. Or place your hand palm forward, with the fingers just touching the back rim of the largest cup, tipping your hand toward the cup so the

Squawk completes stacking cups.

second-largest cup will slide into the larger one. After about the second time of doing this, you can switch to just indicating the larger cup, and usually your bird will catch on quite quickly. Then place the third largest cup in the center of the table and have your bird bring it to you. Just indicate where he is to place it. Repeat with the smallest cup. When he is doing this readily, place the cups in a row, according to size. Have him pick up the second-largest cup and place it into the largest cup, which will be right next to it. Then have him pick up the next cup in line and place it in the stack, and finally the smallest. Birds seem to like this trick and will catch on quickly. Again, this trick, once learned, will require no command or signal. Just place the cups on the table and watch your bird perform.

To make this into an advanced trick, mix up the order of the cups so your bird has to learn to judge sizes to know which cup will go into which other one. But don't try this yet; this is for very advanced birds!

COINS IN A BANK

Description: The bird puts coins in a bank.

Prerequisite: The *retrieve,* as learned in chapter 6.

Equipment: Make or find a piggy bank (see the directions in chapter 13). The main consideration is to have the slot of the bank wide enough to take coins easily. The bank should be sturdy enough so that it doesn't tip over, and preferably have flat sides. Any type of appropriately sized coins will work.

Instructions: Start with the good old *retrieve* exercise of having your bird first bring you a selection of coins from the table. Use the *bring it to me* command and hold your right hand out palm up on the table to receive the coins. Next, holding the bank steady with your left hand tell the bird to "bring it to me," but this time have your hand slanted toward the coin slot opening so the coin will slide from your hand into the bank.

Have your hand slanted toward the coin slot opening so the coin will slide from your hand into the bank.

Remember to have the opening wide enough to receive the coin easily. Let your bird see and hear the coin drop into the bank. Don't forget to P&R each little step. Give a little less help each time until your bird tries to put the coin in by himself. At first, your bird may drop the coin on one side of the bank or the other. Hand the coin back to the bird and tell him to try again or "do better." Do so at first with an excited tone of voice, like "oh, almost, try again" or "hey, you can do better" and then be real excited when he finally gets it into the slot. This is where voice control becomes so important. If you were constantly telling him "no" and handing him back the coin, your bird would soon become discouraged and give up trying. But by acting excited and subtly helping him by tipping the bank or doing whatever is required to help him get the coin in, you will keep his interest up and keep him trying. Like the *ring on the peg* trick where the bird feels the tip of the peg with his beak and so knows exactly how to place the ring, the bird will feel the edge of the slot with his beak and so learns exactly where he must be to place the coin correctly. After he learns that connection he never forgets it, and henceforth, will be able to place anything into a slotted prop. Then you can change from a flat-sided prop to a regular piggy bank, or anything else you might find, to make this into an interesting trick. Let your imagination go, and you will be surprised by what you can come up with.

There is no physical or verbal cue needed with this trick. The prop becomes the physical cue and whatever you want to say, like "bring me the coin" or "put the coin in the bank," works just fine.

Variation One: Distinguishing Coin Sizes

One of the variations you can use to make this trick more interesting involves teaching your bird to distinguish different size coins. Hand your bird a penny and give him the signal for "no." He will shake his head, which usually causes him to drop the coin as though he doesn't want it. P&R. Next hand him a nickel and then a dime. Signal him to shake his head and drop each one. Finally hand him a quarter and have him accept it and deposit it in the bank. Your bird will soon learn to tell the difference in the coins, and will drop each coin without prompting until he receives the "right" one. You can even teach your bird to peek into the bank before depositing the coin.

Variation Two: Putting Coins into a Safe Deposit Box

In another variation, my bird accepts money in return for giving the person a fortune written on a piece of paper, fortune-cookie style. She takes the money and puts it into a safe deposit-like box that has a key in front. I ask her to bring me the key, which she does. Then I open the box and dump the money onto the table. Then she has to pick all the money up and put it back into the now open safe, close the safe, and then lock it. This is chaining tricks together to make a more interesting presentation. You can see how all these tricks are something you can do and also how many tricks are based on the *retrieve* concept you learned in chapter 6.

Kiri, an African Grey, puts a coin into a safe deposit box.

Using her key, Kiri opens the safe deposit box.

Look at all that loot! What can I buy?

LETTER IN A MAILBOX

Description: The bird puts a letter in a stand-up mailbox.

Prerequisite: The previous *coins in a bank* trick.

Equipment: This prop is a miniature version of the mailbox that stands on street corners. The slot is in the front of the mailbox. This is the type of prop you may be able to find in a toy store or thrift store.

Instructions: Start with the mailbox on its back so the slot is in the same position as it was for the piggy bank. Make some "letters" of appropriate size for your bird to carry and to fit into the mailbox slot. At first just have the bird bring you the letter. P&R. Then request him to mail the letter by indicating the slot he should put it in. If he has learned the *coins in the bank* trick thoroughly, he should not have a whole lot of trouble finding the mail slot.

After he knows how to mail the letter, start raising the mailbox up slowly, making sure that he successfully mails the letter each time. Finally place the mailbox in its upright position, which will require your bird to have to work a lot harder to be able to mail the letter.

Poopsie shows how she mails a letter.

PUZZLE BOARD—LEARNING SHAPES

Description: This trick uses a board with shapes cut out of it. The bird must place the correct shape in the corresponding cut out.

Prerequisite: The *retrieve,* as learned in chapter 6.

Equipment: The three most common shapes are the round piece, the square piece, and the triangle. Each piece has an eyehook screwed into the center of it to enable the bird to pick it up. Directions for making the puzzle board are found in chapter 13.

Instructions: First let your bird practice bringing each piece to you as you name it. Say "bring me the *round* piece" and have your hand palm up in the familiar *retrieve* signal. Start with the round piece as it is the easiest shape for the bird to put into the cutout. When he will pick up each shape readily and bring it to you, then introduce the puzzle board containing the cutout shapes. Put the triangle and the square into their respective spots, leaving only the round cutout open. Have your bird bring you the round shape. Indicate where you want him to put it.

Keep saying "bring me the *round* one," so he will continue to hear the name of the shape as he picks it up. P&R. Do this several times until he readily brings you the round shape and places it into the correct spot. Do the same with each of the other shapes. Then your bird is ready for the next step. Remember to always P&R after each little success.

Poopsie now knows the trick and easily puts puzzle pieces into the correspondingly shaped cutouts.

Squawk getting guidance on placement of the round puzzle piece.

Start with the round piece again, but this time do not have the other two pieces in their respective spots. Instead cover the spots with clear plastic wrap so they will appear to be open, but the bird cannot place a shape in them. Then ask the bird to bring you the *round* shape, again emphasizing the name of the shape. Help your bird at this point to learn the names of the shapes by not having the other two shapes out as yet for him to see. Only have the round shape available for him to pick up and bring to you. When the bird brings you the round shape he has to make a choice he did not have before. Now he can see the other two spots that appear open. He might try to put the round shape in one of the other two holes. The plastic wrap should prevent this, but try to gently guide him to place it in the correct spot by tapping the round hole. Then, of course, P&R. Continue to have him bring the round shape until he does so readily and places it correctly, ignoring the other two spots.

Then switch to the square shape, emphasizing the word *square* as you ask him to "bring me the *square* one." Remember to uncover the square hole and to cover the round one now with clear plastic, so he can put the square shape only in the square hole. Finally work with the triangle.

When your bird can bring each shape as called for and place it in the correct hole, make it just a little harder for him. Remove the clear plastic covering from all of the holes. Now when he tries to place the round shape in another hole, a part of it will go in but not exactly fit. Urge him to keep trying and again tap the correct hole to show him where it should go. Then give lots of P&R when he finally gets it into the correct one. Keep repeating with the round shape until he can place it fairly consistently.

Do the same thing with the square shape next and finally the triangle. At this point keep removing the pieces he has already put in so that he has to make a choice each time he tries. This is not an easy trick, so keep working at your bird's pace. If he seems to lose interest, stop when your bird has had some success so you can P&R, and then come back and try again another time when your bird is fresher. Remember, a behavior will be repeated only if it has been positively rewarded in some way.

The final step to making this a complete trick is to put all three shapes out together and have the bird respond to your command to bring whichever one you call for and then place it in the correct hole. When your bird can do this easily, you can be proud. You have trained your bird well to do a fairly complicated trick! This is a major accomplishment!

THE SHELL GAME

Description: In the *shell game* the bird must choose the correct shell under which to find a hidden object. This is a fun trick based on an old game that used to be played at carnivals. People would bet on which shell the object was under. In teaching this trick, we cheat a bit by secretly labeling the shell the object is under so the bird will always know which shell to select, even if his audience does not.

Prerequisite: The *retrieve,* as learned in chapter 6.

Equipment: You will need three identical objects to use for the shells, like walnut halves for very small birds, small cups for slightly larger birds, and progressively larger containers for the largest birds. I have found the plastic tops found on cans of aerosol spray or the larger plastic tops from spray paint cans seem to work fine. All three "shells" must be of identical shape and color. Screw an eyehook into the top of each. Then place a large black dot on the top of just one of the three "shells."

Instructions: Have your bird practice bringing you just the shell marked with a dot, so that he will pick it up readily. Next put his treat under the shell. Let him see you do it. Tell him to "bring it to me." Often when he sees the treat, he will stop and eat the treat first. That is okay; he doesn't have to bring the shell to you anymore. All you want him to do is to start recognizing which shell his treat will be under. As soon as he gets the idea of a treat being under a shell, stop asking for him to bring it to you. That command was used only in the beginning to get him to pick up the shell.

Now add a second shell that is not marked. Your bird might make a mistake and pick up the wrong one, but that is okay. What you want him to learn at this point is that only the marked shell will have a treat under it. Encourage him to try again. Praise him when he selects the correct shell. You do not have to reward him now as he has already gotten his reward from under the shell. When he consistently goes to the correct shell, add the third unmarked shell. Always let him see you place the seed under the shell. Be sure to switch the shells' placement on the table and in relation to each other so the bird does not accidentally learn a position placement. When he is readily selecting the correct shell each time, raise the difficulty by making the black dot on the shell just a little smaller, and then just a little smaller again, but not so small yet that it is difficult to see at a glance.

Now start making your bird work just a little harder. Let him see you put the treat under the shell, but then mix the shells around. Now he has to really look for the shell with the black dot, the nearest one will not be it anymore. But he will catch on pretty quickly; he wants that treat!

If you have not already done so, introduce a table perch at this point. What it amounts to is a station that your bird must go to between tricks. Before now it has not been as important, but from now on you don't want your bird to be standing right over the shells as you mix them up. The table perch gives your bird a place to go to between repetitions.

Up to now your bird has gotten his own treat by lifting the correct shell. Now you are going to change the criterion. Find a small object to which you can attach a wooden knob or screw eye that will fit under the shell. A small white bottle lid works well. Make it small and flat enough so that your bird doesn't have to lift the shell very high to get it. Have your bird bring it to you a few times and get rewarded for

Kiri finds the "shell" with a seed under it.

Giving It Away

If you want to make the *shell game* trick seem more credible, make sure your bird is watching you as you place the lid under the shell and then mix them up. In one show, Kiri, my African Grey, had just finished a successful selection of the correct shell, and I had praised and rewarded her and sent her to her perch. I then proceeded to place the lid under a shell and mix them up, explaining all the while that the birds could do this trick easily because of their wonderful eyesight, when I heard a few snickers from the audience. I finished the shell placement and then turned to Kiri to start her on her next selection when there she was, completely facing in the opposite direction, eating her seed and paying no attention to the shell placement at all. I learned in a hurry to always keep an eye on my bird and make sure she is at least facing in the right direction to help give my lines some credibility.

it so he will recognize its value as a treat getter. Now add this part to your shell game. When he picks up the designated shell, he will see the lid instead of his usual treat. Use your *bring it to me* command and flat hand signal to tell the bird to bring you the new object that is now under the shell. When he does, of course P&R. Send him to his table perch and then repeat the trick, letting him see you place the new object under the shell, and then proceed to mix the shells up.

He will shortly accept this new step before getting his treat. Then you can raise the criterion one final time. Make the black dot smaller and smaller until it is just barely a speck. You can even use a ballpoint pen to make a small dot. You can stop using any commands or cues for this trick as soon as he understands what he is to do. You can say things like "which one do you think it is under now?" Your bird will proceed without further prompting. When he masters all this, you have completed another good trick.

RINGING A HANGING BELL

Description: The bird goes to a bell and pulls a bell cord to make it ring.

Prerequisite: The *retrieve*, as learned in chapter 6.

Equipment: For this trick you will need a bell on a stand with a cord attached to the clapper. Remember the little white plastic rings you can find in most sewing notion stores? You were told to practice with them when teaching the *retrieve*. Now, here is another place to use them. Attach one of the rings to the end of the cord attached to the clapper on the bell.

Poopsie rings the bell by pulling the small ring on the cord.

Instructions: Ask your bird to "bring it to me." If you have trained your bird well in the *retrieve*, when he sees your flat hand, palm up, he will immediately start looking for something to bring you. He should recognize that plastic ring he had brought you before, which is now attached to the bell's clapper. He will probably try to beak it a little to see whether he can bring it to you. Even touching it just a little will probably cause the bell to make a small sound. Encourage that with P&R, letting your bird know he is doing something right. Your bird will undoubtedly try taking the plastic ring again. Each time encourage him by saying "bring it to me," and he will soon be grasping the ring and giving it some good pulls. This is an easy trick to teach, and one birds seem to like. My Blue-crowned Conure especially liked this one and would go to the bell unbidden any time she saw it and pull the cord again and again just to hear the bell ring.

RETRIEVING A DUMBBELL

Description: In this trick the bird picks up a dumbbell you have thrown and returns it to you. This trick will be especially fun for those who have trained dogs in obedience work using a dumbbell.

Prerequisite: The *retrieve*, as learned in chapter 6.

Equipment: A small dumbbell the appropriate size for your bird. Directions for making a dumbbell are included in chapter 13.

Instructions: Put the dumbbell on the training table and ask your bird to "bring it to me." The only part you might have to train is showing the bird how to pick up the dumbbell in the center as he might try to pick it up by one end. But holding the dumbbell by the ends and presenting it to him so he has to take it in the center usually solves that problem quickly. He will soon find it is more convenient to pick it up that way. Make it a game by tossing the dumbbell onto the table and then making a big fuss over him when he brings it to you.

RETRIEVING A DUMBBELL OVER A HURDLE

Description: Your bird jumps over a hurdle, picks up a dumbbell, and then returns it to you. Again, you'll enjoy this trick if you've ever trained dogs for the obedience ring.

Prerequisite: The previous *retrieving a dumbbell* trick.

Equipment: This trick needs a small bar or solid type hurdle. Do not use your table perch; the hurdle is to jump over, not to perch on, so don't confuse your bird by using the table perch.

Instructions: Start with the hurdle very low so your bird can actually step over it. Then raise it up just slightly so your bird has to make a little effort to step over it. Never allow him to put a foot on or step onto the hurdle. You might want to use a word like "jump" to get him to go over it on cue. This is not always easy, but have patience and you can usually get your bird to jump a little. Place the hurdle in front of you and the bird on the far side and ask him to "come." As he approaches the hurdle, say "jump" and make a fuss over him if he even tries. Only after he gains that skill should you add the dumbbell, placing him and the dumbbell on the far side of the hurdle facing you, telling him to bring the dumbbell to you using the *retrieve* words and signal.

When your bird can do that, place the hurdle at right angles to you with the bird and the dumbbell to your left. Use the same *retrieve* words and signal but hold your right hand flat on the table to your right, coaxing the bird to jump perpendicular to you this time instead of to you. Reverse positions and this time have the bird jump from your right to your left. You now have the beginning of the *retrieve over a hurdle* as done in dog training. Have the bird on your right and place the dumbbell on the far side of the hurdle to your left. Tap the dumbbell with your hand or the target stick and encourage the bird to jump. When he gets over the hurdle, if he is at all hesitant about what to do next, use your *retrieve* cues and tell him to "bring it to me." It won't take many repetitions before he will know that after he jumps the hurdle he is to pick up the dumbbell and carry it back over the hurdle, without additional cues and signals.

Poopsie is performing this trick familiar to dog obedience fans. She is carrying the dumbbell over a hurdle.

You can make interesting variations of this by having a higher hurdle and letting the bird jump onto it and then immediately continuing to the other side. Or even better, using the higher hurdle, have him jump one way and then go under it carrying the dumbbell on the return.

LIFTING A BARBELL

Description: The bird picks up a barbell and then lowers and raises it.

Prerequisite: The *retrieve*, as learned in chapter 6.

Equipment: For this trick you will need a barbell, which is just a little different than a dumbbell; mainly the crosspiece is longer and there are balls on the ends instead of blocks of wood as on a dumbbell. Instructions are given in chapter 13 on how to make one.

Instructions: Have your bird pick up the barbell with the *retrieve* command, but instead of letting him bring it to you, use the target stick to tap the table as though asking him to touch it. He will probably lower his head to do so. Immediately tell him "good," but don't offer a reward. Catch him before he releases the barbell. Repeat the action a few times until the bird understands all he has to do is raise and lower his head while holding onto the barbell. The barbell becomes the cue, no other is needed.

Cassie is showing off a bit by hopping around with this barbell.

A variation of this trick is teaching your bird to turn around or hop with the barbell. Have the bird do the *turn around* on the table top instead of on a perch. Then present him with the barbell. This time when your bird picks up the barbell, don't let him lower it as before. Give him the signal to *turn around*. With a little bit of coaxing, you can pretty easily get him to continue holding the barbell as he turns around.

To make the trick even funnier, I also give Cassie, my Black-headed Caique, the signal to hop, which is an innovative trick, explained in chapter 10, "Innovative Tricks." When you do any combination often enough it soon becomes the whole trick, and the separate parts don't need cueing. Now when Cassie sees the barbell she runs over, picks it up, and begins to hop up and down in a circle with it.

Chapter 8

Advanced Tricks Based on the Retrieve

As in the preceding chapter, all of the following tricks are based on the *retrieve* concept taught in chapter 6, "Teaching the Basic Retrieve Command." Do not attempt to teach these more advanced tricks until your bird really understands this concept and has mastered at least some of the tricks in the previous chapter. The following tricks are heavily dependent on props. I will tell you either how to make some of the simpler props or where you can shop for them in chapter 13, "Making Props." For the more elaborate props, you will have to use your own creativity and resources.

In the following section, you will learn to train your bird to pull something behind him, like a wagon, as opposed to the next section, in which you learn to train your bird how to push something ahead of him, like a grocery cart. Each of these two skills—pull and push—is taught separately, but many tricks can then be taught quite easily based on these concepts.

PULLING A PULL TOY

Description: The bird pulls a pull toy to where you designate.

Prerequisite: The *retrieve,* as learned in chapter 6.

Equipment: You will need a white plastic ring with a piece of string tied onto it and a small pull toy with wheels that is appropriate to the size of your bird.

Instructions: Start teaching the pulling concept with a simple pull toy. Take one of those handy white plastic rings we used in teaching the *retrieve* and tie a 6-inch (or longer, depending on the size of your bird) piece of string to it. Have your bird

Poopsie, a Green-cheeked Conure, demonstrates learning to pull a toy with a string and ring attached. She is asked to "bring it to me."

practice his *retrieve* skills by bringing this ring with the string attached to you. Have him *retrieve* this ring until he no longer is concerned by the dragging string. Then pick out a simple pull toy with wheels. Attach the free end of the string to the pull toy.

Now lay the string out on the table with the toy attached and put your hand on the table just a little ways away. Using the *retrieve* cues explained in chapter 6, tell your bird "bring it to me." He should pick up the plastic ring immediately and try to put it in your hand. Go slowly if he is at all intimidated by the pull toy moving. Give him lots of praise and reward (P&R) if he pulls the string at all. Keep moving your hand a little farther away each time he is successful and encourage him to pull the toy just a bit farther. Soon the toy on the end of the string will no longer bother him, and he will be pulling it the length of the table.

PULLING A WAGON

Description: The bird pulls a wagon to a designated location.

Prerequisite: *Pulling a pull toy,* as described in the previous section.

Equipment: Little red Radio Flyer wagons, miniatures of the toys sold for children, come in several small sizes and are commonly found in many places from toy stores to hardware stores. To turn one into a bird prop, you must alter the length of the wagon tongue. Remove the handle from the wagon tongue and then take a piece of hollow rod and fit it over the remaining tongue. Make it fit tightly. The length of the tongue needed will depend on the size of your bird and the length of his tail. Then put a small rod crosswise through the end, making it whatever length is necessary for your bird to pick it up easily. Your bird will usually prefer to pull the wagon on one side of the tongue or the other. Allow him to choose which side he prefers.

Instructions: With the prop prepared, use the *bring it to me* command and cue for your bird to bring you the wagon. It is very important to the success of all the tricks in this chapter to have a solid foundation in the *retrieve* (see chapter 6). Your early efforts will really pay off as your bird learns these advanced tricks.

Have your bird pull the wagon from left to right across the training table. Place the wagon to your left and place the bird behind the crosspiece on the wagon. Then put your right hand in the now familiar *bring it to me* position, with the palm up, a little ways to your right in front of the bird and ask him to "bring it to me." You might even pick up the crosspiece to encourage him to take it in his beak to bring it to your hand. He will probably do so readily. He might not even need your help if he has learned many of the beginning tricks shown in chapter 7, "Simple Tricks Based on the Retrieve." For a finished trick, ask him to pull the wagon all the way down the table.

To make this wagon trick a little fancier, I taught Squawk, my Blue-crowned Conure, to unroll a "red carpet," which I explain later in this chapter. Next I fitted a wooden dowel crossways into the bed of the wagon and placed Cassie, my

Cassie, a Black-headed Caique, pulls a wagon loaded with her toys.

multitalented Caique, onto the dowel and told her to "stay." Telling Squawk to "bring it to me," she easily pulled Cassie and the wagon down the length of the red carpet to make a triumphal entry with Cassie on her first try.

VARIATIONS OF PULLING A WAGON

Try these variations of pulling a wagon:

- Have two birds each pull a "chariot" across the floor in a race to see who wins.

- Have your bird pull a wagon filled with his sports equipment to a "play-field" and have him play such games as basketball, baseball, or "fetch" with the props he brought in his wagon.

- Combine the push and pull concepts. Have your bird load a wagon with, maybe, miniature sacks of birdseed. Then have him pull the wagon to a station and unload the bags of feed into a pushcart. Finally, have him push the cart to a designated place. *Pushing* is taught in the next sections.

PUSHING A GROCERY CART

Description: This is the opposite of what your bird does in the previous tricks. Instead of being in front of the object and literally pulling it along behind, in these tricks your bird gets behind the object and pushes it ahead of him. Here, the bird pushes a grocery cart to some grocery shelf props and takes some of the groceries and puts them into the cart. Then he pushes the cart home.

Prerequisite: The *retrieve,* as learned in chapter 6.

Equipment: Little grocery carts used in this trick are frequently found in novelty or home stores and sometimes on the Internet. You'll also need some "groceries," often found with doll accessories or other miniature items.

Instructions: Position your bird behind the cart and tell him to "bring it to me." It's that simple. If your bird is at all afraid of this prop, or any other prop for that matter, condition him first by letting him look at the prop, be around it, and see how his trainer seems to either ignore it or play with it. Sometimes you can put the new prop on one corner of the table and just work around it while practicing other behaviors. Soon the new prop doesn't seem as scary. And after you have used many such props, your bird will take it all pretty much in stride. Eventually when he sees a new prop, he will not be afraid of it, but will just wonder what his owner has in store for him this time. My birds all accept new props now with hardly any concern. But it wasn't always that way. So watch the reaction of your bird to a new prop and wait to use it until he is ready.

African Grey Kiri pushes her grocery cart.

When your bird first starts trying to push the cart to you, reward him every time he makes even a little progress. Each time reward him for pushing the cart a little bit farther. After he brings the cart to you, start having him push the cart across the table from right to left and back again. Just the placement of your hand, palm up as the signal, as you did in teaching the *retrieve,* will usually cause the bird to bring the cart to wherever you indicate.

If you really want to get fancy with this trick, have your bird make a turn while bringing the grocery cart to you. This is quite a bit harder for your bird to do, compared to just pushing a cart in a straight line. Have your bird start pushing the cart from left to right. Then at about mid-table give the *bring it to me* cue so your bird has to turn the cart toward you. Help your bird at first by having him turn the cart in a wide turn, not a sharp one. You will find your bird makes the cart turn by going to the outside of the handle and pushing it from there. You can help him turn the cart by having him take that position on the end of the cart handle, and from there, he can learn to turn the cart on his own. After a few tries, your bird will automatically move his grip on the handle to the outside when he turns it.

Being able to turn the cart can make this into a nice trick. From having the bird just push the cart in a straight line, now he can turn it to a place where you have placed some "groceries." You can make some small grocery shelves, use doll house furniture, or use a small table to put some groceries on. Your bird will bring you the grocery cart, then pick up the groceries one by one and place them into the cart. With your bird's now finely tuned *retrieve* skills, it is no big deal to indicate to your bird to "bring it to me" for the groceries, and then just tap the cart to indicate where the bird is supposed to put the groceries. You can add to this trick by turning the cart around and having your bird push it back to where he started from and then unload the groceries.

This is an example of how you can chain tricks together to make a simple trick into a more complex and more interesting final trick. I have devoted chapter 11, "Chaining Tricks," to this subject and will discuss this trick further in that chapter.

PUSHING A BABY CARRIAGE

Description: The bird pushes a baby carriage to a cradle and takes the baby from the carriage and places it into the cradle.

Prerequisite: *Pushing a grocery cart,* covered in the previous section.

Equipment: A baby carriage appropriate to your size bird. Small baby carriages are usually easy to find in doll stores, craft shops, and even thrift shops.

Instructions: After allowing your bird to get used to the prop, place him behind the carriage and give him the *bring it to me* cues. He should have no trouble figuring out what you want him to do if he can do the *pushing a grocery cart* trick. If not, start him exactly as outlined in the previous section and reward him for each little move he makes pushing the carriage to you. Then have him push it from right to left across the table and then back again. Finally have him try to push the baby carriage in a rounded path to you.

To make this trick more interesting, hand your bird a "baby bird." I've used one of those yellow chicks you can sometimes find in Easter baskets, but any small object your bird can hold easily in his beak you can call a "baby bird." Ask him whether he would like to take the baby for a ride and hand him the baby. At first you might have to indicate by tapping on the baby carriage where he is to put the baby. Then to make a nice ending you can have him push the carriage to where you have a cradle and ask him to put the baby in the cradle. Again. you use the *bring it to me* command and cue to ask your bird to pick up the baby, and then by tapping on the cradle show him where to put the baby. When the trick is learned, your bird will readily take the baby and place it in the baby carriage; you will no longer have to indicate where he should put it. The same with the second part of taking the baby from the carriage and placing it in the cradle. A nice finish to this trick can be added by having your bird place a foot on the cradle, and then by pressing up and down, rock the cradle.

You can break this trick into smaller parts by having your bird learn to push the baby carriage first. Then have him just take the baby and put it in the carriage. Repeat this segment until he understands it. Then have him bring you the baby

Poopsie is training to become a nanny.

from the carriage, and finally place it into the cradle. When he can do all the parts separately, you can put it all together. When your bird is first learning, be sure to P&R each part as he masters it, but when you are working on the finished trick, have him do all the parts in order before he gets his P&R. Verbally encourage your bird, tell him to keep going, and encourage him to keep trying to do better. Be effusive with your praise when your bird has done a good job. Birds are very auditorily oriented and will soon pick up all your nuances of instruction and praise. Your bird will respond quickly to the pitch, tone, and cadence of your voice.

PUSHING A BALL

Description: The bird moves a ball, like a miniature bowling ball or soccer ball that he cannot pick up, by pushing it with his beak.

Prerequisite: The *retrieve,* as learned in chapter 6.

Equipment: A small soccer ball, a bowling ball, or even a plain solid wooden ball will do. Do not use a plastic ball unless it is fairly heavy.

Instructions: This concept is not too difficult to teach after your bird knows the *retrieve* thoroughly. Mainly it involves asking your bird to bring you a ball that he cannot pick up. Place this ball on the table and ask your bird to bring it to you. Your bird will attempt to pick the ball up as he has done with other balls before, but since he cannot pick up this ball, he will only succeed in rolling it around a bit.

At first reward your bird for just rolling the ball around with his beak, but then subsequently reward him only when he succeeds in rolling the ball a bit toward

Poopsie pushes a ball with her head and beak.

you. It won't take many repetitions for your bird to learn he is rewarded only when he pushes the ball to you. You might want to add the verbal command of "push" at this time. Remember to say the command in a light, encouraging tone, as in "push, push, good boy!" Use the command only as a teaching concept and for use with future tricks. After a trick is learned the *push* verbal cue is not necessary. Usually the props used become the cue.

When your bird understands pushing the ball, ask him to push the ball from a greater distance each time. Then ask that he push the ball from left to right and reverse, across the table, to wherever you place your hand in that familiar palm up *retrieve* position. Be sure to do that with any of the *retrieve* tricks so your bird won't associate retrieving objects with just bringing them to you. He must bring them to wherever you designate. Now he is ready to learn some tricks using this new concept.

BOWLING

Description: The bird pushes a ball into bowling pins.

Prerequisite: *Pushing a ball,* covered in the previous section.

Equipment: A solid, fairly heavy ball and a set of bowling pins. A bowling alley is an added bonus. A bowling alley could be a wooden channel slightly elevated on one end for the ball to roll down.

Instructions: One way to perform this trick is to have your bird simply physically push the ball into the pins, knocking them over. Another way is to make an alley (see picture) to help guide the ball to the pins. By slightly raising one end of the alley, you will ensure that the ball will roll into the pins on its own. Place the ball at the upper end of the alley and ask your bird to give the ball a push with his head to get the ball started rolling. If you have been practicing having your bird pushing a ball from left to right and then the reverse to your hand, cueing your bird to give the ball a starting push down the alley is very easy. Position the ball and the bird at the upper end of the alley. Use the *retrieve* physical cue of the hand with the palm up while saying the verbal cue "push." Your bird will almost certainly try by beaking the ball, thus causing it to roll down the alley. The ball will strike the pins, and you can delightedly P&R the bird.

To add interest to this trick, have your bird follow the rolling ball, walking down beside the alley to the pins. Be sure to place the pins so that there will always be one or two left standing no matter where the ball strikes. Then request that your bird knock over the remaining pin or pins by giving him the *retrieve* cue. Let him only pick up standing pins. P&R him when he first starts to pick a pin up; he doesn't have to bring the pin to you, you only want him to knock them down. So when he picks the first pin up, P&R him immediately and ask him to pick up another. It won't take long before he realizes he is getting rewarded for only touching the pins and thus knocking them over, not for bringing them to you.

After your bird can do all of these things easily, you can add this piece to make it into an even more interesting trick. Find a receptacle you can place the balls in, something to replicate the containers that hold the balls at a bowling alley. Find a wooden bead the size of the bowling ball you have been using in training. Hammer a weight into the center of the wooden bead to give it a little more stability

Kiri demonstrates how to get the ball rolling in a game of bowling.

when rolled. Because of the hole already in the bead the bird can, with a little effort, pick this ball up. Ask him to bring the ball and place it at the top of the alley, again using your *retrieve* command. Then tell him to give it a push down the alley as he has done before. Let him proceed to finish the trick by knocking down any pins left standing. You might want to require him to send two balls down the alley, as in a regular game, before finishing the trick.

Add each part gradually, and only after the preceding part has been thoroughly learned. At first P&R after each part, but after your bird has learned the steps, P&R only after the entire trick is performed. After the trick sequence is learned, you will need no cues or signals; the bowling prop itself becomes the physical cue. As a warning, do not use the final bowling ball with the hole in it for teaching any other part of the trick. The bird must not be able to ever pick the ball up in the beginning learning process. You might, however, paint the ball you use as the final bowling ball the same color as your initial training ball so that he will understand he must also push this last ball after placing it at the head of the alley. Then if you wish to add a second ball, now that your bird has accepted the first one, you should be able to paint this second ball any color you like.

SOCCER

Description: The bird pushes a ball down the table through goal posts.

Prerequisite: Knowing how to push a ball with his beak, covered previously in this chapter.

Equipment: For this trick you will need a small soccer ball, found in many sizes in novelty stores. You will also need something to use as uprights, or goal posts. I

Cassie playing soccer.

found it easiest to start with a board that I painted green to simulate a playing field and added a pair of goal posts at one end with a crosspiece connecting them. (More directions are given in chapter 13.) Some fake birds that you can weigh down so they stay in place make good interceptors and are a fun addition.

Instructions: First start with your bird as in the *bowling* trick described previously, just pushing the ball to you. Then have him push the ball back and forth across the training table to your hand, or to where you indicate. Then introduce your soccer field prop with the goal posts and ask that he push the ball to your hand through the posts. From now on insist that your bird always push the ball through the posts to get his P&R.

When your bird is readily doing this, remove your hand as a cue to where he is supposed to push the ball and indicate through the goal posts only when necessary. Soon he will be pushing the ball on his own through the posts. Next make it a little more difficult by placing the ball at different positions on the field so he must now guide and correct his pushes to get it through the posts. When he understands what you want and can do this easily, place some obstacles in his way, such as the fake birds that are weighted to stay in position. Place them in such positions that your bird has to maneuver the ball to get around them to get to the goal posts. Cheer him on each time he gets around an "interceptor," but do not stop the action by offering a reward. Reward him only when he gets the ball through the posts. Keep changing the fake interceptors' positions so your bird really has to develop his skills. This makes the game just a little more challenging and interesting to watch. Finally, you might want to add having the bird jump or climb to the top of the goal posts, perch on the cross bar and take a bow, or maybe flap his wings in triumph after he has scored a goal. When he's done all this, be sure to really jackpot him by offering extra treats.

Poopsie Plays Soccer

I have produced a series of videos/DVDs in which my birds do tricks and I instruct viewers how to train their own birds. In my first video, I show Poopsie, my Green-cheeked Conure, pushing a lawn mower on a soccer field to get it mowed and ready for a game. The soccer field prop is a piece of wood painted green with goal posts installed at one end. Poopsie has to push the lawnmower down the field, turn it around, and then push it back between the goal posts and off the field. She plays soccer by pushing a ball down the field using her beak to push and direct the ball between and around fake bird defenders until she finally pushes it between the goal posts. For a finish she hops up on to the crosspiece between the goal posts to take a bow.

ROLLING OUT A CARPET

Description: The bird pushes a rolled-up piece of material out flat, to imitate a walkway carpet.

Prerequisite: Any of the *push* tricks from this chapter.

Equipment: Fashion your mock carpet from a piece of felt or other material, as wide as the bird needs to walk on easily and cut it a little shorter than the length of your training table.

Instructions: This trick is easy to teach if you have schooled your bird well in the *push* tricks taught earlier. Roll the "carpet" up tightly but leave the trailing edge out so your bird can step on it to start the trick. He needs to stand on it so his weight will keep the entire roll from moving and allow him to just start unrolling the rest. Place it on the table with the bird and carpet to your left. Use your *retrieve* palm up signal but use the verbal cue of "push." Your right hand should indicate that he is to bring it across the table to your right. If he has learned the previous exercises well he should understand immediately what you want and start pushing the carpet roll. Encourage him to push the carpet all the way open before he gets his final treats. This is not too much to ask at this level of training. Use your imagination to decide what you will use the rolled-out carpet for. As I mentioned earlier, I had my Conure bring out a wagon with my Caique perched on it and pull the wagon down the red carpet.

Squawk, a Blue-crowned Conure, is ready for royalty and will give them VIP treatment.

RAISING A FLAG

Description: The bird grabs the end of a cord attached to the flag and brings it to you, thus causing the flag to be raised.

Prerequisite: Mastering *pulling a pull toy* will make learning this trick a lot easier.

Equipment: The prop consists of a flagpole with hooks inserted to allow a pulley system to raise a flag attached to a cord. Attach a white plastic ring to the open free end of the cord. This is a familiar prop for your bird to retrieve that you learned about in chapter 6.

Squawk pulls a ring to raise the flag.

Attach the flag to the cord at whatever is the highest point involved in raising it. Then bring the flag to its bottom position. The flag is raised by pulling on the ring at the end of the cord.

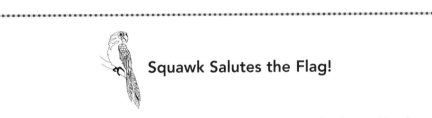

Squawk Salutes the Flag!

Squawk, my Blue-crowned Conure, has an innovative trick of scratching her head on cue. (See chapter 10, "Innovative Tricks.") She will readily follow my hand motion of lifting my hand to scratch my head by lifting her foot to do the same. But I noticed she seemed to be following the movement of my hand so if I didn't put it all the way up to my head to scratch, neither did she. So I got the idea of only putting my hand up to my head as in a salute and then she would do the same. From this a nice trick evolved. She raises the flag, and then I pick her up and give her the signal of my hand going only to my temple, as in the salute gesture, to indicate to her she is to raise her foot only to her head, to appear to be saluting the flag.

Squawk shows how she salutes the flag.

Instructions: There are other ways to raise a flag, but the way described here seems to be the easiest. Ask the bird to "bring it to me," using the verbal and physical *retrieve* cues. Since the bird now is very familiar with the cue and has seen the small white plastic ring before, it is very easy for him to comply. He should pick up the ring and bring it to you at once and so easily raise the flag.

CARRYING A BANNER OR A ROD

Description: The bird carries a banner or a rod from one place to another. I distinguish between *banner* and *rod* by referring to a banner as a short piece of dowel with a sign attached hanging down from the center, and a rod as a longer piece of wood or wire with something, like pennants or flags, attached to the ends. In this trick, the bird must hold the center of either the banner or rod in his beak to balance it while carrying it.

Prerequisite: The *retrieve,* as learned in chapter 6.

Carrying a Banner

Equipment: You'll need a short piece of dowel from which you can hang a banner. Carrying and displaying a banner is best suited for larger birds. However, a small or short-legged bird could learn to hold one while sitting on a perch or from a perch held up in the air.

Instructions: Start with a short piece of dowel and ask your bird to bring it to you. This is really just an extension of the *retrieve* with the same cues used except

Cassie lifts the flag from the table while hanging upside-down.

now you are going to hand your bird a dowel rather than have him pick it up off the table. Teach these tricks in the order shown because if you try to teach him to take something from your hand right after teaching him to bring you something from the training table, it can confuse him. You want your bird to always look for something to bring you from the table when given the retrieve cues.

At this point, with good solid experience bringing you things from the training table, it will not be too big a step to let your bird take something from your hand on occasion. So hand him the short piece of dowel, and P&R when he brings it to you. When your

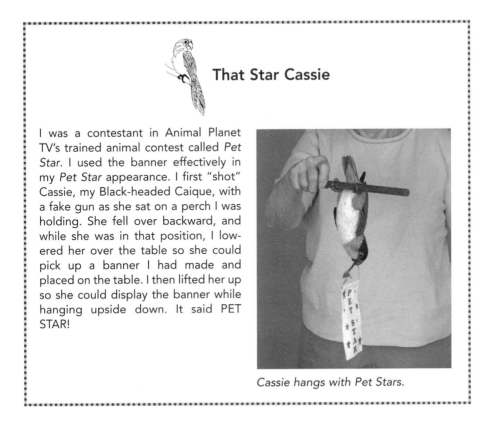

That Star Cassie

I was a contestant in Animal Planet TV's trained animal contest called *Pet Star*. I used the banner effectively in my *Pet Star* appearance. I first "shot" Cassie, my Black-headed Caique, with a fake gun as she sat on a perch I was holding. She fell over backward, and while she was in that position, I lowered her over the table so she could pick up a banner I had made and placed on the table. I then lifted her up so she could display the banner while hanging upside down. It said PET STAR!

Cassie hangs with Pet Stars.

bird will take a shorter dowel from you and will carry it the length of the table, add a piece of material or paper, or something to it to make it into a banner, which is just a piece of wood with a sign attached. Have your bird then practice the *stay* command taught in chapter 4, "Necessary Obedience Skills (Husbandry Behaviors)," while holding the banner. It makes a nice ending to a show to have your bird walk toward the audience holding a banner with appropriate wording, and then stop and just hold the banner in front of himself so the audience can read it.

Carrying a Rod

Equipment: A rod is a piece of wood or wire with something like pennants or flags attached to its ends. The bird must hold the center of the pole in his beak and balance the two ends while carrying it.

Instructions: Basically the same as for teaching *carrying a banner*. Make the rods you hand him of different lengths so he learns to bring you any size you give him. He must hold the rod or the banner exactly in the center to be able to balance it. Then start adding objects to the rod ends. Wrap material around the ends, hang pennants from the ends, or attach small flags that stick up from the ends, all different things. Eventually your bird will pay no attention to what you place on the ends of the rod. It will become just another "thing." Have some things hang down from the rod ends while other things go up. Remember to practice having your bird carry the rod from one side of the table to the other, not always just to you.

Variation: Walking a Tightrope Carrying a Rod

You might want to add a "tightrope walk" to the trick. String a cord, a rope, or a cable between two upright posts strong enough to hold the tightrope steady. Have a platform attached to each upright. First have your bird walk back and forth on the rope from one platform to the other, until he becomes confident enough for the next step. Then hand him the short rod and let him carry it while crossing the

rope. As he succeeds make the rods longer and start adding different things, as suggested previously. Pennants are always effective. I remember once I was asked to put on a show at a luncheon that was using a patriotic theme. For a final trick I attached a small flag to each end of the pole, and my bird carried the flags across the rope to the tune of "It's a Grand Old Flag." That trick was an instant success!

Flags are attached to the rod Squawk is carrying on a tightrope.

CHANGING A MARQUEE

Description: The bird goes to the marquee and changes the sign. I use the marquee signs between each bird's appearance in my show. Each bird changes the marquee before her part, to introduce herself and give the audience her name and species. I also use marquee signs in my videos/DVDs, not only to introduce my birds, but to let my audience know what trick will be shown next.

Prerequisite: The *retrieve,* as learned in chapter 6.

Equipment: I use a suspended three-hole notebook and let the bird flop the sign down from the upside of the notebook. Now with computers it is so easy to make big legible signs for this trick.

Instructions: Suspend the notebook with just one page in the upper position. Hold your bird in front of the marquee and tell him to "bring it to me." With only the page in front of him to grab a bird usually tries that immediately. And voilá, he gets P&R. A few repeats, and he has the idea. Then put your bird down alongside the marquee and again give the *retrieve* cues. He now has a pretty good understanding of what you want, so he usually reaches over and pulls down the page fairly readily. If not, just indicate the page with your hand or target stick and he will get the idea.

Cassie introduces her part of the show.

Some fun things to add to make this trick more interesting are variations on your bird's approach to the marquee to change it. I have Kiri, my African Grey, roller skate to the marquee to introduce her act. Poopsie, my little Green-cheeked Conure, has to climb a small stepladder to even reach the marquee. Use your imagination and make it fun.

DISPLAYING A SIGN

Description: The bird releases a sign while standing above it, and it falls into position for the audience to view. Or the bird can pull a sign down into position while standing under it.

Prerequisite: The *retrieve,* as explained in chapter 6.

Equipment: As in many of the tricks in this chapter, obtaining the props is the main problem; however signs for this trick are not too difficult to make. I started out with a small roller shade I had cut to size and taught the bird to pull it down. I used that small handy plastic ring I keep mentioning and affixed it to the middle of the shade.

Instructions: Using the *retrieve* cues, I asked the bird to "bring it to me." I started out with a very small, very short sign so it was not difficult to operate, and my bird could lower it easily. You know the progression: Make the next one a little bit bigger, then a little bigger, until any applicable size will be grasped and lowered.

Cassie pulls this sign down to end the show.

You might prefer a drop-down sign. Attach the sign to a wood base. Then roll it up and wrap a ribbon around it. Next tie that little plastic ring to one end of the ribbon and nail the other end of the ribbon to the wooden base. Finally nail a small short headless nail into the top of the wooden base and put the plastic ring over it. Now it is just a matter of teaching your bird to remove the ring from the base and thereby release the sign. You can guess how to do that by now. The good old *retrieve* cues! Your bird will try to bring you the plastic ring—the only possible thing in sight for him to try to bring you. Of course in doing so the plastic ring comes off the nail, and the sign drops down. Your bird will probably be very startled at first, but after much praise and a reward he will probably be willing to try it again. Soon it becomes quite easy for him to do.

You can get quite creative in displaying your signs. One idea is to put the sign on a tree branch and have your bird fly to or climb to it to release the sign for a dramatic touch to start your show. Or build a platform to suspend the sign from and have your bird climb up to the platform, by rope or pole, to release the sign. Use your imagination to make things enjoyable! Trick training and showing off tricks can be a lot of fun.

PUTTING A HAT ON A RACK

Description: The bird picks up a hat and places it on a hat rack.

Prerequisite: The *retrieve,* as learned in chapter 6.

Equipment: Choose a small hat your bird can pick up easily that is not too floppy. A stiff plastic one is a good choice. Make sure the hat will go onto a hat rack easily. If not, put a wire on the underside of the hat across the crown. (Simple directions for making a hat rack are given in chapter 13.)

Instructions: Lay the hat topside up on the table. Have your bird at first bring you the hat by the brim. Then add the hat rack and ask your bird to now bring the hat to you and place it on the rack, which you are holding. Using the *retrieve* cue, have your hand flat, palm up, on the rack to show your bird where he is to place the hat. He will lift the hat. You can now see the

Putting a fireman's hat on a rack is no problem for Squawk.

wire on the underside of the hat. Help him at this point by manipulating the rack so that it will snag the wire and, thus, the hat will be hung on the rack. P&R after each successful attempt. Use your voice to keep him trying to place it and reward only when he is successful. Start with the hat rack not too high off the table so that at first placing the hat will be easy. Then when your bird has the idea of where to put the hat, you can start raising the rack gradually to its final position, which should be just high enough so the bird has to reach up to place the hat on the rack.

OPENING A MAILBOX

Description: Use a small version of a regular rural-type mailbox. To obtain the mail the bird must first lower the flag on the outside of the box, then open the door to the box, and finally take out the mail and bring it to you (you're the one who can read!).

Prerequisite: The *retrieve,* as learned in chapter 6. The bird should be comfortable retrieving pieces of paper.

Equipment: Small rural-type mailboxes seem to be easy to find at variety stores. Attach the box to a secure base so the height will be compatible to your bird. Fold some paper into the appropriate shapes to simulate "letters." You can even address them to make them look the part.

Instructions: Have the flag on the mailbox in the up position. Ask your bird to "bring it to me" and indicate the flag. Loosen the screw that holds the flag onto the box so that it will fall very easily. Your bird will most likely touch the flag as he knows he is to bring you something. The flag will fall and you P&R your bird. In about two repeats he will realize that touching the flag generates treats. Then tighten the flag screw slightly so he has to work just a bit harder to get the flag down. The trick is still easy for him to do, and he will probably do so readily. Tighten the screw only until the flag will stay up, but not so much that it will take any big effort to lower it. Then move on to the next part.

If you have not practiced with your bird in bringing you pieces of paper when you were teaching the *retrieve,* do so now. Make up some paper to look like mail envelopes. Put them on the training table and ask your bird to bring them to you. When he does this readily, place the bird in front of the open mailbox where he can see the mail. Have the door to the mailbox open and flat. Put the mail on the door to start with so it will be easy to see and easy for the bird to pick up. Ask him to bring the letters to you. You can indicate the letters by tapping them if he does not go to them at once. When he touches the letters or picks them up, P&R him. Each time he is successful put the mail a little farther into the box until he has to actually reach inside the box to get the mail. He knows that retrieving the letters is now what earns him rewards, so he will try hard to get them and bring them to you.

Next close the door just a little so your bird has to reach into a slightly smaller opening to get to the mail. P&R each time he is successful. Keep closing the door just a little more each time until the bird finds he has to actually push on the door to get to the mail. You will find as you keep closing the door, that he will almost impatiently push the door down to get to the mail. Soon you will have the door

It's time to check the mail.

Some of the tricks on these pages are not taught in this book but are included here to inspire you to use your imagination and invent new combinations.

Cassie, a Black-headed Caique, has to reach to make the basket.

Poopsie, a Green-cheeked Conure, is so little she needs a ladder to reach the hoop.

This was an easy trick for Cassie to learn since she likes playing on her back.

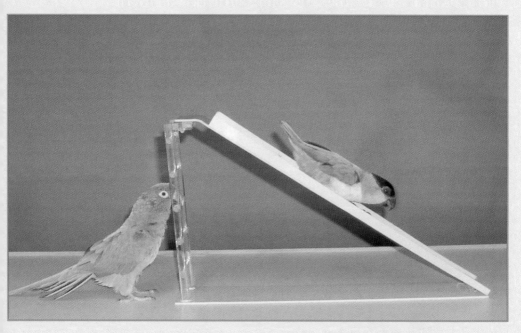

The slide trick is not based on any other trained behaviors.
This was one of the more difficult tricks to teach.

Peekaboo, I see you! Hanging by your feet and then sticking your head through the ring is not an easy trick to do.

Cassie enjoys riding on her truck.

Cassie shows that she knows her colors by
placing a blue ring on a blue peg.

Squawk, a Blue-crowned Conure (left), is a little heftier than
Cassie (right), so Cassie uses physics and moves down on the
teeter-totter to make her side go down.

In this trick, Squawk goes through a tunnel.

Charlie, a Blue and Gold Macaw, raises his wing when he
wants to ask a question.

Don't play tic-tac-toe with Poopsie—she always wins!

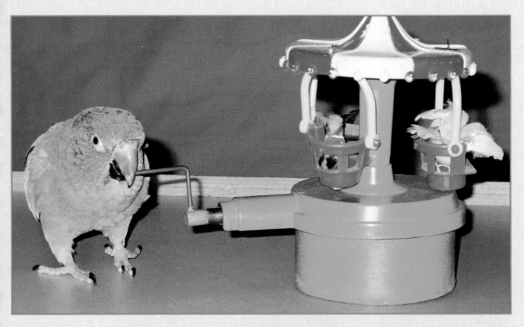

Squawk gives her friends a ride on the carousel.

Kiri, an African Grey, likes to read while relaxing in
her favorite lounge chair.

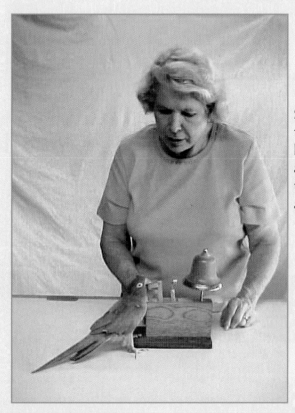

Squawk gives the answer
to simple math questions
by pulling on the bell the
appropriate number of
times. This is another very
advanced trick.

I've got a job for you and your wheelbarrow, Kiri.

Squawk likes a bottle before taking a nap.

all the way in the up position but not latched, and the bird will be able to open it. That deserves much P&R!

Another way to teach him to open the mailbox is to actually put his treat inside the mailbox. He will very quickly figure out how to open that door when a treat is inside.

Only after the bird understands that he must open the door to get the mail or his treat, should you attempt to latch it. This makes it a lot more difficult for the bird to open the mailbox, but if he is physically capable of it, after repeated attempts and lots of encouragement on your part, he should be able to do it. Loosen the latches, separate them slightly, or do whatever is necessary to keep them from latching too tightly.

Now you have a chained trick. You ask your bird to bring you the mail. He goes to the mailbox, lowers the flag, opens the door, and brings you a letter or two. I know in real life, the mailman is supposed to lower the flag when he leaves mail, but for the purposes of this trick we pretend he forgot to do so. You can stop here if you want. It is a good trick. But if you want to really make it fancy, you can chain more of the same behaviors, in reverse, to demonstrate a complete mail cycle.

After you take the last letter from your bird, you can then ask your bird to mail a letter from you. Hand him a new letter and indicate he is to put it into the mailbox door. Remember each trick your bird learns makes learning the next trick easier. So understanding where he is to put this new letter should not be difficult for your bird. Remove any previous mail from the box so he does not become confused as you teach this next part. Now you are going to teach him how to close the mailbox door. Having it almost closed to start with helps. Tell him to push with his beak, just as he did in the earlier *soccer* and *bowling* tricks, and help him to do so. Lower the door just slightly each time he is successful until it is all the way down and he is pushing it closed readily.

Now he must learn how to raise the flag on the side of the box. Target the flag, and when the bird touches it, help him raise it and praise him as though he was doing it all himself. For some reason, raising the flag to the up position is not hard to teach as the bird is used to seeing it in the up position. He seems to understand that is where it should be. Again, make the flag very easy to move so it will take very little effort on his part to move it.

Now start putting the trick together. With the mailbox open, hand your bird a letter and ask him to mail it for you. He should immediately take it to the box and place it inside—that is the easy part. Then request he close the door. When he does that, remind him to put the flag up. At first P&R each part. When he can do the whole chain, reward him only after he completes the whole trick.

Now that he has all the parts to the trick you can start from the very beginning. Ask your bird for the mail. He pulls the flag down; then he should go to the front of the box and open the door. He then brings you the mail. Then you hand him a new letter and ask that he mail it for you. He takes the letter, places it in the mailbox, closes the door, and raises the flag.

Your bird has just completed a fairly complicated, chained trick. Be proud!

RIDING A SCOOTER

Description: The bird propels himself down the table holding onto the handle of a scooter with his beak, keeping one foot on the base of the scooter and using the other foot to push on the table.

Prerequisite: The *retrieve,* as learned in chapter 6.

Equipment: You will need a scooter of a size that your bird can push and maneuver easily. It's also helpful if your training table has an edge around it so your bird doesn't become frightened by accidentally scooting off your table.

Instructions: Birds are right- and left-footed just like we are right- and left-handed. Let your bird make the final choice of which foot he wants to place on the base of the scooter and which one he wants to put on the floor to push with. You can usually tell which foot he favors by watching which side of the scooter the bird initially goes to when he tries to push it to you.

Don't be discouraged if it takes your bird awhile to learn this trick. Start by placing the scooter in its upright position on the table and asking your bird to bring it to you using the *retrieve* cues. Your bird will probably think you have gone

Riding a scooter becomes an alternate form of transportation.

Fast Learner

Squawk learned this trick in about fifteen minutes, but of course, she was well schooled in other tricks first and knew the *retrieve* concept well. I placed the scooter on the table and told her to "bring it to me" using the *retrieve* verbal and physical cues. She looked around and saw only the scooter on the table so she, of course, knew that it was what I wanted her to bring to me.

First she got in front of it and tried dragging it to me. That didn't work too well, so then she got behind it and tried pushing it to me. I encouraged her to keep trying with my voice. Squawk is way beyond the stage of needing to be praised for every little step like first approaching the scooter, then grasping the handle and trying to push or pull it to me, and so on. These are separate actions deserving a reward if she were a less experienced bird. But being experienced, she knew she was supposed to bring me something and that when she did she would be rewarded. Finally I decided to help her so when she was behind the scooter trying to push it, I gently placed her one foot on the base, leaving the other foot on the floor. I called her again. She gave a push with the foot on the floor to try and come to me. The scooter moved forward easily, and she got the idea. Soon she had pushed it to me to get her P&R.

mad, but maybe he will at least approach the scooter. For the inexperienced bird, go back to rewarding each little baby step. He approached the scooter, so P&R. Give the command again and don't P&R until he has at least touched the scooter, then P&R. Next try to get him to do something with the scooter, anything, in an effort to bring it to you. He is now beginning to see the scooter as his treat getter (the source of rewards) and knows he must do something with it to earn them. The bird will usually try to grasp it in the hope of dragging it to you. That is a positive step, so P&R, but next time insist he actually move it a bit toward you before getting his reward.

After letting him try that a few times, gently place him behind the scooter to see whether he will try pushing it to you. When he does, be sure to P&R. And only P&R again when he is in this pushing position. You are being selective in rewarding only the positions and moves that will lead to success. Finally when he has succeeded in pushing the scooter a bit toward you, gently lift his leg and place it on the scooter. P&R when your bird allows you to do this. P&R again for keeping his foot on the base. Your bird does not necessarily have to break position to get his P&R. Use your voice to encourage him to keep trying. When he keeps his

Squawk has to pick the scooter up in order to ride it.

foot on the scooter base and the other on the floor, he will soon get the idea of trying to step forward with the floor foot, which will make the scooter move. Praise and reward him profusely—give him a jackpot! Trainers use this word as a verb, too, as in "jackpot your bird." This means give extra treats and, of course, much praise. Your bird will understand that pushing with one foot on the table and another on the scooter is now how he is supposed to bring you the scooter. It will be just a short time until he is able to ride the scooter across the table to you.

This trick needs no verbal or physical cue. The scooter is the cue itself.

To make this trick more challenging, have your bird pick up the scooter that is lying on its side and ride off with it. Hold the scooter at just a bit of a downward angle on the same side your bird rides it. Ask him to bring it to you. He will have to right it to be able to ride it, and it is just amazing how quickly a bird can figure this out. Keep lowering the scooter with each success. Find something to lay it on so you are no longer holding it. Keep putting it lower on the table until you are finally able to lay it all the way down on its side. The bird will have to pick it back up to its upright position in order to ride it. I even deliberately put the scooter down on the opposite side from which my bird rode it to see what she would do. She picked the scooter up and then hesitated only a second before she stepped across it to be on her preferred side to then ride it off. The intelligence of these birds never fails to amaze me.

RIDING A SKATEBOARD

Description: This trick is similar to the *riding a scooter* trick, except there is no longer a handle for your bird to grasp. Your bird must push a skateboard with his one foot on the table and then balance himself with the other on the skateboard.

Prerequisite: The *riding a scooter* trick, covered in the previous section.

Equipment: A skateboard that is wider than the scooter and has both ends turned up.

Instructions: There are pluses and minuses to teaching your bird how to ride a scooter before teaching him how to ride a skateboard. The scooter is easiest for the bird to learn because he can grasp the handle of the scooter and balance easier in what can be an awkward position. The downside is that the bird becomes dependent on that handle. Your bird might try to grasp the front of the skateboard with his beak and ride it that way. And, usually, your bird is able to do so. But, of course, it looks funny and is not the way you want to see your bird ride the board. Make sure that the skateboard is much wider than the scooter, just as real ones are, so the bird cannot grasp any of the base with his foot to try to hold on.

Place your bird on the same side of the board he preferred when riding the scooter and ask him to bring it to you. You might help him to stand on the skateboard if he seems at all reluctant. There is nothing wrong with using physical assists when appropriate. You might even want to move the board forward slightly to help him get started. If your bird has been well schooled in riding a scooter, he will understand at once what is required; he will usually just want something to hang on to. Again, don't let him grasp the front of the board! Help him to make even small pushes with his feet at first and give him lots of encouragement for doing so. Hold his treat up in front of him so he will try to move forward to get the treat with his head up. It might take a little time, but it is worth the effort. Soon he will be pushing the board as readily as he does the scooter.

When your bird is riding the skateboard easily, you might like to try adding a ramp. Start off with a board just slightly slanted. Then you can raise it by small increments to the point where your bird will put both of his feet on his skateboard and glide down. Give him plenty of run-off room and watch to be sure he doesn't end up sliding off the table. You're his spotter for this trick.

Riding a skateboard is fun!

Squawk Has a Memory Like an Elephant

I was putting on a show in Houston. I had arrived a day early so I could get set up and run through some of the tricks ahead of time. Squawk had just mastered the skateboard and ramp so this was to be her first show using it. My training table at home has a small lip all around the edge to keep things from rolling off. It's also useful as a stop for the skates, bicycle, scooters, and so on. But I wasn't using my training table in Houston. I was using the regular banquet table that was furnished by the hotel. I set up the ramp and placed the skateboard in position at the top. Squawk walked up to the top of the ramp and got on the skateboard as planned with no help from me. Off she sailed and was gliding nicely. The board kept on going right off the end of the table. Squawk, being a bird and built to fly, didn't just drop like a rock; fortunately, she was able to save herself from serious injury by flapping her wings. But did she ever lose confidence in me! She was not about to try the trick again. It had to be dropped from that show.

Of course, when I got her back home I was able to practice the trick and start with her back on the flat, then adding the ramp as her confidence increased. Soon she was performing as well as before. The interesting part of this story is that I went to Houston again the next year for a show. I had forgotten about the incident and just had absorbed into my subconscious the need to always give enough run-off room to prevent accidents. I did not need to have a practice ahead of time so just proceeded into the show. Imagine my surprise when we came to the part where she was to climb onto the ramp to get on the board, and she refused to do it. Now Squawk is a well-seasoned show bird and had never refused any trick I have asked of her before. She had been riding the skateboard successfully and easily for almost a year. I couldn't believe it. I finally picked her up and placed her at the top of the ramp. She still refused to get on the board. She actually remembered that hall and what had happened there a year before. Unbelievable! I might add, she has never refused to do the trick at any other place.

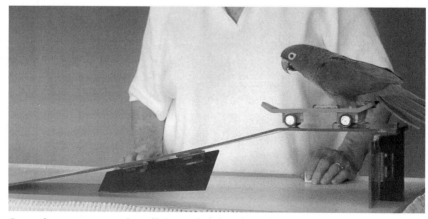

Squawk prepares to take off down the skateboard ramp.

TURNING A CRANK

Description: The bird grasps a handle and turns it. This concept can later be applied to any number of props that have cranks to turn them.

Prerequisite: The *retrieve,* as learned in chapter 6.

Equipment: You will find quite a few toys that have cranks, just be sure to get only ones with cranks that turn easily. Potential crank props to look for include a cash register with a crank that when turned will open the cash drawer, a merry-go-round or Ferris wheel that is turned by a crank, a jack-in-the-box, or a wishing well with a crank-operated bucket. A good source is a thrift shop that has many inexpensive toys with which you can experiment.

Instructions: Place the handle of the crank toy in the straight up position. Place your bird behind the handle and then cue him to "bring it to me." All your bird can see is that handle, so usually he will tentatively reach for it. Target it with your hand or stick so he will touch it. When he does, P&R him. Encourage him to bring it to you and usually the bird will respond by taking hold of it and trying to move it. The handle will do the only thing it can do and fall forward. P&R him. Do that a few times and your bird will see that doing things with that handle results in a treat, so he will keep trying to do something with it. When he pushes it forward readily, move the handle a little bit more toward the bird than straight up. When he successfully pushes the crank forward and down, keep moving its starting position to more and more toward the bird so now he has to lift it

Here we go round and round . . .

slightly to get it to go forward. Finally the handle will be in the almost down position. When your bird gets the idea he now has to lift and then push the handle around to get his treat, he is almost there. Next encourage him to push the handle around again. Do not reward him when he has turned the crank once but insist he try it again, and reward him when he has completed a second revolution. Soon you can ask him to keep cranking until you tell him to stop. Keep your request reasonable.

Chapter **9**

Miscellaneous Tricks

This chapter deals with various tricks, some of which might be a little more difficult than others. The more experience your bird has with learning tricks, the easier each successive trick will be to teach. First teach your bird as many tricks as you can from the previous chapters and then progress to work on some of the tricks in this chapter.

In writing this book, I grouped similar tricks together or those of similar difficulty. That does not mean they should necessarily be taught in the order presented. As pointed out in this chapter, do not teach the *roll over* immediately after teaching your bird to play dead. In the same vein, do not teach the *somersault* at the same time as you teach the *roll over*. Remember that each trick your bird masters will make learning successive tricks much easier, but as he learns more tricks and cues, it also become easier to confuse him with similar cues. Make sure one trick is thoroughly learned before introducing a similar one.

PLAYING DEAD

Description: The bird lies on his back on the table and remains in that position until released.

Prerequisite: A bird should be well-socialized and accept handling. The bird should be at number 6 on the Tameness Scale discussed in chapter 2, "Preparations for Training."

Equipment: No props are needed for this trick, just treats and patience.

Instructions: In the beginning, as you were socializing your bird, you should have been gently tipping him onto his back in your arms and cuddling him like you would a baby. With your smaller size bird, hold him in the palm of your hand.

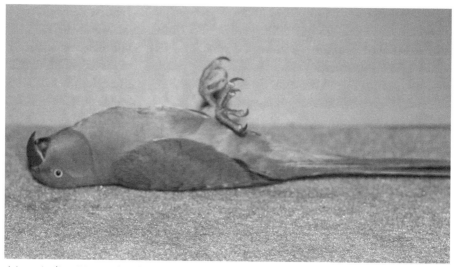

AJ, an Indian Ringneck, plays dead.

Let him see that being on his back is not so scary. Remember, this is not a natural position for most birds, and they can be quite resistant to it. Some species, like Caiques, flop over quite readily and like to play with each other and their toys while on their backs. But for most birds, being on their backs is frightening. Take it easy when teaching this trick so you don't unduly alarm your bird.

The next step is to put your bird on his back in your lap and play with him there. Only after the bird is used to being held on his back and is comfortable with it should you put him down on the training table. At first, put him on the training table on his back for just a few seconds. Then pick him up and praise and reward (P&R). Do this a few times until he can relax enough for you to take your hands away and leave him in that position for a short while. This is a big step for some birds, so don't rush it.

Next have the bird roll away from you and get up by himself. But allow him to get up only on your command. Make him stay lying on his back until you give the release command of *okay*. Even then insist that he get up by rolling over away from you. This is laying the foundation for the *roll over* trick that follows next. But for now the bird must learn to remain on his back until released.

The last step is teaching the bird to lie down on his own. That is the biggie. Up until now you have been putting him down on the table on his back. Now he must learn to lie down on his own. Start with the bird on the training table facing to your right. Grasp his tail feathers with your left hand and gently turn him over, turning him first onto his left side and then onto his back. He should end up parallel to you with his feet to your left, his head to your right. Some birds seem to feel more secure if they can hang onto something with their feet as they lay down. If so, let him grasp the fingers of your hand or a short piece of wooden dowel as you help him to lie down. When he is on his back, at first it helps to gently hold him and encourage him to stay in that position until he is comfortable. If he has been in that position before on the table and found that he got praised and rewarded profusely for lying there, he probably will not protest too much. If your bird still wants something to grasp while on his back, after weaning him from holding onto your fingers, let him hold a couple of his own tail feathers. That usually helps in the beginning stages of training this trick.

Give your release command of *okay* and help him to get up by rolling him away from you. Put your left hand under his side and push gently as he gets up. Then P&R. Do not give him a food reward while he is on his back as that might encourage him to get up before he is released, but do praise him for the position and for remaining there until released. Then P&R after he is up. Keep repeating the sequence until he will lie down on his own and stay until released.

One common physical cue you can use to tell your bird to play dead is to pretend to shoot your bird by pointing your index finger at your bird. Give the physical signal just before you help the bird to lie down so he will associate the signal with the act. I would not add a verbal cue, something like "bang, you're dead," until after the bird is well trained for just the physical cue. You might want to think up something more original, or have the flexibility of saying something different each time. Really, the physical cue is all you need.

To make the trick cuter and more original, I point at the bird and say something like, "Which would you rather be, a Democrat or a dead bird?" That's an attention grabber, especially if it's an election year. You can think up all sorts of questions that can be answered by your bird playing dead. The physical cue, pointing at the bird, remains the same for any question.

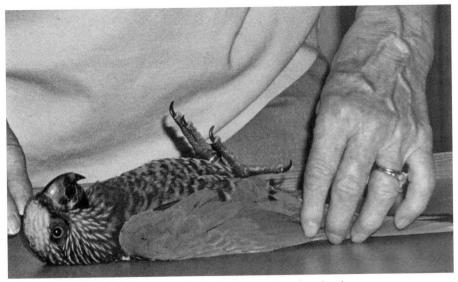

Xena, a Hawk-headed Parrot, is physically assisted to play dead.

Jazz It Up

If your bird likes to hold something in his feet, you can use that need to enhance your trick. For just the *play dead* trick, I give Kiri, my African Grey, some daisies to hold, and say she is "pushing up the daisies." For Squawk, my Blue-crowned Conure, I have her lie on a small bed and then I hand her a baby bottle to hold while she is "taking her nap." For Cassie, my Black-headed Caique, I pretend to make a "parrot cocktail" out of her by placing her on the top of a cocktail glass and handing her a prop "olive" to hold (see chapter 11). Just use your imagination and you can come up with all sorts of things to make the act of your bird lying on his back into a really cute trick.

Kiri is "pushing up the daisies" while playing dead.

ROLLING OVER

Description: On cue the bird lies down and immediately rolls over in one continuous motion.

Prerequisite: *Playing dead,* as taught in the previous section.

Equipment: A safe flat surface for performing the trick, and lots of treats and patience.

Instructions: Don't teach this as a separate trick until you have been doing the *playing dead* trick for quite some time, and your bird is quite reliable. You don't want to confuse your bird, as these are two separate tricks. Start by giving your bird the *play dead* physical cue, but as soon as he is down, give the signal to *roll over.* This is the right index finger, held parallel to the table pointing at your bird's face, making a small roll motion similar to the roll over motion your bird will be making. At the same time, use the left hand to help him to continue his roll as you did previously in helping him get up from the *playing dead* trick. What differentiates this trick for your bird is that you now say "roll over" as you signal your bird to lie down, and there is no praise given while your bird is on his back. He is helped to *roll over* as soon as he lies down. Try to make the action continuous with no pause while he is on his back.

As soon as he starts to get the idea of what you want him to do, drop the pointed index finger that you use as a cue in the *playing dead* trick, and go to using the cue of the index finger making a small rolling motion as you say "roll over." Give help only as needed but be quick to do so if the bird hesitates or doesn't seem sure of himself. And as always, give lots of praise and rewards when the bird successfully completes a trick.

SOMERSAULT

Description: This trick is always a crowd pleaser. In the finished trick, the bird will put his head between his legs, roll forward onto his shoulders, then his back, and then over his tail to again land on his feet in one continuous motion.

Prerequisite: You should be able to handle your bird all over and roll him around with your hands. (For milestones in the socialization of your bird, refer to the Tameness Scale discussion in chapter 2.)

Equipment: No props are needed, just a safe flat surface.

Instructions: The cue for the somersault is the forefinger held parallel to the table, in front of your bird's face to start with, pointing away from your bird, and moved in a forward motion, simulating the somersault movement you want the bird to make. The finger is perpendicular to your bird's face as opposed to the cue for the *roll over,* the trick taught previously, in which the finger is pointing at the bird. Use the verbal cue of *somersault.*

You can do a lot of prep work for this trick, especially with a younger or small bird, by rolling your bird over in your hands during the taming play stages prior to the more formal trick training done on the training table. To a bird who is used to being held upside down, and turned around in your hands, this trick is easy to teach.

To start the formal training of the *somersault,* place your bird with his left side to you on the training table. Cup his head in your right hand and gently bend it forward and down. When your bird no longer objects to this being done, proceed to roll him gently onto his shoulders, then his back and finally onto his feet again. Use the left hand to help where needed. If you do the physical manipulation carefully and gently, letting

Cassie being taught how to do a somersault.

Look at Me!

I will never forget when Cassie first "got it." I had been working on her *somersault* on the training table for some time helping her to do it when I got a phone call that I decided to take. Taking the call would give Cassie a breather, I rationalized. The phone is right next to the training table, so I did not have to leave or get up to take the call. But I did stop paying attention to Cassie for the moment. Then I noticed her, and here she was, doing a *somersault* all by herself, looking at me to see whether I was watching, and then doing another and yet another. She was trying to get my attention again by showing me she could now do the *somersault* all by herself. I think she had understood the trick for some time but enjoyed my attention and praise and physically handling her. I imagine she thought I was playing with her still as I had held her and rolled her around in my hands many times before in play during the socialization process. Anyway, I couldn't help but laugh and quickly ended the phone call to give my undivided attention to Cassie again. It was a win-win situation.

your voice tell him all along what a good bird he is, you probably won't have too much resistance from him. You can see now why all the socialization and handling was so important to do before you started trick training. Don't skip that step! The positive side is that you are going to end up with a wonderfully tame and compliant pet for the many years ahead.

Just keep physically assisting him to do the *somersault* over and over with lots of P&R, and he will eventually understand what you want him to do.

A future application for this trick is to hold the bird on your finger and have him do a *somersault*, or a forward roll as I sometimes call it, around your finger.

Cassie performs a forward roll (somersault) around Tani's finger.

Combine that with other tricks that can also be done on your finger, such as the *wave, turn around, nod head yes, shake head no, shake hands,* and give a *kiss* (all covered in chapter 5, "Tricks That Don't Require Props"), and you have a nice little grouping that your bird can easily do on your finger any time and any place. You can still do similar groupings with the larger birds from a floor stand.

HEADSTAND ON TABLE

Description: In this trick the bird stands on his two legs with his head between his legs, looking like he is standing on his head. This trick is always a crowd pleaser. Because of their longer legs, larger birds seem to be able to do it more easily.

The headstand performed on a table.

Prerequisite: The bird should be well socialized and accept handling.

Equipment: No props are required to perform this trick.

Instructions: When the bird puts his head between his legs for the *headstand,* the legs, of course, are helping to balance him. Start with your bird on the training table with his right side toward you. Place the target stick between the bird's legs from behind his back and encourage him to touch it. As the bird reaches down for it, give P&R. In small increments, gradually move the stick backward, between the bird's legs, asking him to touch it each time you move it. Parrots can quite easily put their heads all the way down through their legs and reach under their tails. When the head is in the position you want, ask the bird to hold that position for a second or two before you give him the release command of "Okay." Gradually require him to hold the position for a second or so longer until he will hold it until you release him. You do not need a physical cue for this trick; merely put him in position and start to lower his head. He usually takes it from there, but you can add any verbal cue you wish, such as "Can you show us how you stand on your head?" as you put him into position.

HEADSTAND ON HAND

Description: This trick differs from the previous one in that the bird balances on his shoulders and head on your hand, rather than with his feet and head on a table. Doing this trick depends on your hand size and the size of your bird. If you can hold your bird easily on your hand, you can do the trick.

Prerequisite: The bird should be able to do a *headstand on table.*

Equipment: No props needed.

If you can hold your bird on one hand, he can perform a headstand on it.

Instructions: Place your bird with your left hand onto your right hand, held palm up, onto his shoulders with his head forward in front of his shoulders. He is actually balancing on both his shoulders and head. Cup your right hand so he is also supported by your fingers and slowly get him to balance on your right hand alone by carefully removing your left hand. This trick does not seem to be hard for birds to do, especially after having learned the *headstand*. As your bird gets used to the position, you can slowly begin to straighten out the fingers of your right hand so he is now balancing just on your outstretched hand. It's kind of a cool trick that the bird can learn really quickly.

CLIMBING A LADDER

Description: Climbing a ladder (or other objects such as a rope, a pole, or rings) usually involves your bird climbing from the training table or the floor to a specified place, such as a platform, perch, or even his cage. You seldom have to teach this skill as birds usually learn it on their own just playing around their cages.

Prerequisite: None.

Equipment: Get a sturdy ladder that is appropriate to the size of your bird. A bigger bird will take a heavier ladder, with rungs spaced further apart, and a small bird needs a smaller ladder with smaller rung size for his smaller feet. Start with a fairly short ladder, and then as your bird becomes more experienced, you can graduate to a longer one.

Instructions: This trick is especially easy to teach as it takes advantage of one of your bird's natural behaviors. In the wild, birds climb all over their surroundings. What you want to do is to teach your bird to climb a ladder on command.

Have the first ladder for your untrained bird go from the tabletop to just the top of his table T-stand. Fasten it to the top of the T-stand so it won't slip. Use the target stick to coax your bird to just put his foot on the lower rung of the ladder. P&R as usual. Then shape the behavior by coaxing your bird to take another step, and then another. Lure him by holding a treat out for him so he has to climb a rung to reach it. In no time he should be climbing a ladder with ease.

Another way to teach this behavior is to put your bird near the top of the ladder and lure him to go up a few rungs to reach the platform or perch and get his treat. Then keep placing him lower on the ladder until he can climb it easily from the very bottom. Regardless of the way you choose to teach this trick, it won't take long for your bird to learn to climb a ladder. No verbal or visual cue is needed. I use a long ladder in my "fireman" trick for my bird to climb way up to the top of the ladder and then transfer over to an equally long metal pole to grasp and slide back down. All the birds I have taught this trick to just seem to love it.

CLIMBING A ROPE OR A POLE

Teaching your bird to climb a rope or a wooden pole is about the same as teaching him to climb a ladder. Choose a rope (or a pole) that is appropriate to the size of your bird and one he won't snag or catch his feet on. Attach the rope to a perch or a platform with which the bird is familiar. Place the bird near the top of the rope so he is just a few grasps from the top. Encourage him to climb to the top by holding a treat out for him. And, of course, always P&R when he succeeds. Place him lower on the rope each time until he is climbing up from the bottom. Use your voice to urge him to continue to climb after he has started up the rope. You do not want your praise to mean he should come back down

to get his reward, but just to tell him that he is doing great and should continue. When he reaches the top, then really P&R. Of course, make the length of the rope climb appropriate to your bird's experience. Increase what you ask of your bird only after he has gained proficiency in this skill. Because birds like to climb, this trick is easy to teach. No verbal or visual cue is needed.

You can use a rope for birds to climb in several tricks. Your bird could climb from the base up to the top of a platform on a rope, and then jump across to another platform and back flip down. Or you could have him climb a pole up to a platform to ring a bell or perhaps release a sign. You will find many uses for climbing a rope or pole, and best of all your birds will really enjoy it.

Cassie climbs up a rope foot over foot.

SLIDING DOWN A POLE

Description: After climbing a ladder, rope, or something similar to reach a high platform, the bird grasps a metal pole and slides back down to the bottom.

Prerequisite: The bird should be comfortable *climbing a ladder* or *climbing a rope* or *a pole* on command.

Equipment: A ladder, a rope, a wooden pole, or something similar to climb up to a platform, then a metal pole attached to the platform, to slide down. Make the diameter of the pole match the size of your bird; the length of the pole should be governed by the purpose of the trick.

Instructions: Luring is perhaps the easiest way to teach this trick. Place your bird on the pole near the bottom, just high enough off the ground so he cannot jump off readily. Hold his treat out to him and encourage him to come to take it. A bird's usual reaction is to loosen his hold on the pole slightly to enable him to jump, and this loosening causes him to slide down the pole slightly, just enough for him to get off. When he does this, give much P&R. Then repeat, each time placing him just a little higher on the pole. In just a few repeats, he will have the idea of sliding, and then he will actually start to enjoy it. If your

bird jumps off too soon, you can tell him "no, do better" and place him on the pole again. Soon your bird will find the slide is the treat getter and when he finds he is not being hurt, he will stay on until he reaches the bottom. Some birds will shift from their tail down on the slide to their face down as they slide. This is okay, too, as long as they complete the slide; it is just a different approach. When your bird can do the whole slide, let him start from the platform at the top and figure out how he is to get onto the pole to start his slide. Most birds will do this readily with little help from you. Then add the trick of your bird climbing up the ladder to the top to start his slide down, and you have a completed trick.

Squawk slides easily down a pole. She has fun doing this trick.

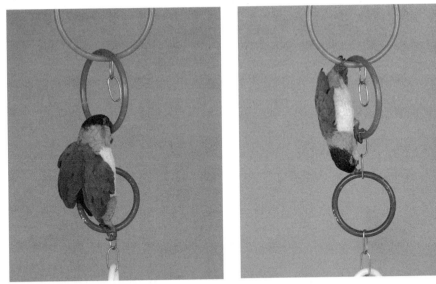

Cassie climbs up and down hanging rings.

CLIMBING RINGS

Climbing rings, a series of plastic or metal rings linked together, is taught in exactly the same way as *climbing a ladder.* Climbing up and down, through and around rings, is fun for your bird and good exercise. Use different sizes of rings so that your bird can climb from one straight up to the next, and then use another size ring for him to have to climb through and perch on before reaching the next ring. I use rings suspended from my hanging cages and let the birds get exercise climbing down to the floor and then back up, two exercises your bird will respond to readily on your directive. No cues are needed, other than indicating what he is to climb.

HAULING UP A BUCKET

Description: This is not a difficult trick and can be a good way to check out your bird's intelligence. Your bird pulls a small bucket or basket up from below him by using his beak and feet to grasp the rope.

Prerequisite: None.

Equipment: For a really professional-looking trick you will probably want to get a prop that looks somewhat like a wishing well. I made mine out of a nut dish and added uprights to it with a perch for the bird to stand on. To teach the trick,

Hauling up a bucket is easy for this Military Macaw.

however, you can make do with just about anything. For the larger parrots you can use their floor stand. For the smaller ones make a bar stand that would be easier to use than the table T-stand. The bar stand is just a base with two uprights that support a bar perch fastened between them.

In addition to a stand on which to perch, you will need some sort of a bucket or basket that is appropriate to the size of your bird. Baskets are best because the bird can easily grasp it in his foot after he hauls it up. The basket should be large enough for the bird to get his head into easily and should not be very deep. I have occasionally seen wooden buckets or even metal ones that larger birds can handle. For the smaller birds, though, you definitely don't want a metal bucket, as it is very difficult for your bird's feet to grasp and hold!

The last prop you will need for this trick is a cord or string to use to attach the basket to the perch. Again the size of the bird will dictate what kind of a cord (or string or rope) you will use. Make sure that whatever you select is safe and that your bird cannot catch a toe in it. This is true, of course, for any toys you ever get for your bird. It's always safety first. The length of the cord should be proportional to the size of your bird. For some of the smaller birds use a cord about 9 or 10 inches long and a shallow basket about 1½ inches in diameter. Increase these sizes for the larger birds.

Instructions: First let your bird eat a few seeds from the basket so he will associate the basket with a treat. Then attach the basket to the cord and let him hold the basket as he eats treats from it. Finally attach the cord to the crosspiece of your stand. Make sure that your bird is able to get his head into the basket easily. Wrap the cord around the crosspiece he is perching on until the basket is suspended just below him. Let him take a few treats from the basket. Then gradually lower the basket by small increments each time he successfully reaches it and gets his treat. Soon he will find that he has to grasp the rope and pull the basket to him to get the treat.

Poopsie learns that the basket holds treats.

As you lower the basket still farther, your bird will find he has to step on the cord and take another grasp, using his beak and feet. This is where you will be able to gauge your pet's intelligence. Some birds get the picture immediately and starting with the rope and bucket at full length; they can figure out what they have to do to get that treat. With little hesitation they start figuring out ways to pull the basket up beak over foot. Other birds take a little longer to get it and need to be trained step by step as just described, with you lowering the bucket slowly as they figure out what to do. But this is not a difficult trick, and your birds can learn it. No physical or verbal cues are needed for this one as the prop becomes the cue.

For fun, try the following variations on this trick:

- Place a ladder against the crosspiece and have your bird climb up to the perch, pull up the bucket, and then climb back down when finished.

- Put an object in the bucket other than his treat and have your bird take that object out and hand it to you before receiving his treat.

- Have your bird bring the object with him as he climbs down the ladder and then hands it to you. Your story could be that something has fallen in the well and he is retrieving it for you.

Let your imagination go, and you can come up with all sorts of ideas.

JUMPING THROUGH A HOOP

Description: When a hoop is held in front of him, the bird jumps through. This is a spectacular trick.

Prerequisite: If your bird has already learned some beginning tricks, it will make it easier for him to learn this more advanced trick.

Equipment: Use a low table stand, the kind that you will want the bird to perch on between the tricks. Use a hoop large enough for the bird to jump through easily. Err on a larger size for the hoop.

Instructions: With your bird on a low table stand, hold a hoop right in front of him and ask him to "jump." You can hold food in your fingers to lure him, or use the target stick for him to touch to get him to get off the perch and go through the hoop to get to the treat. As always, P&R each time he succeeds. Slowly move the hoop a little farther away so he has to jump to go though it. The main thing is not to let him touch the hoop with his feet at any time. If he tries to land on the hoop or touch it with his feet as he passes through, use your disappointed voice and tell him "no, that wasn't right." Give no reward, of course, and then ask him to do it again. Back up a step to where he last successfully jumped through the hoop and start from there.

Cassie jumps through a hoop.

When your bird is jumping from the table perch through the hoop to the table-top, try having him jump from one table perch to another perch of similar height, without the hoop. Place the two perches fairly close together and tap the perch you want him to jump to. When he is doing that readily on the command of *jump,* you can increase the distance between the two perches only to the point where he can jump easily. Then add the hoop, holding it very close to him in between the two perches. With each success gradually increase that distance until the hoop is in the middle between the two perches.

When your bird is jumping readily, increase the distance you are asking him to jump. A clipped, heavy-bodied bird such as an Amazon or an African Grey cannot jump too far, so make the trick for them more spectacular by increasing the height of the two perches they have to jump between.

As a final step for your clipped bird, decrease the size of the hoop until it is just big enough for him to jump through easily. This makes the trick look more difficult.

For your flighted bird, this can be the start of lots of fun tricks. As you increase the distance between the perches, encourage your bird to fly through the hoop to the other perch and then to fly back. As you increase the height of the perches and the distance he is to fly to or from, you will end up with a really spectacular trick. Work on having your bird fly to and from perches, or stations, maybe in a circle through hoops, rather than flying to or from you. Reward your bird for landing on a designated perch. Then *you* go to his perch to P&R. Teach him in

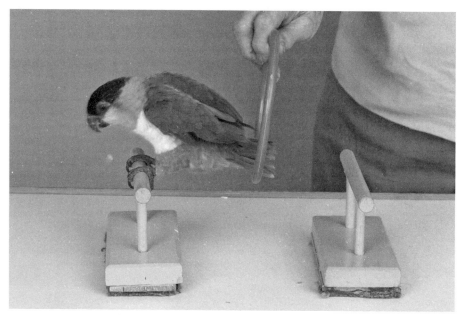

This is a training stage in teaching jumping through a hoop.

this way, instead of letting him come to you and landing on you for his reward. This will save you a lot of grief later on if you should want to expand this trick. You can always have him fly to you as a *recall* later on.

Besides the free-flying through hoops described previously, you can add paper to the hoop and teach the bird to break the paper as he flies through. Do this by making a large gash in the paper so the bird can see his way through easily at first. Then decrease the size of the gash, until it is a small hole. Use flimsy tissue paper to make it easy for your bird to break through.

RINGING A SERVICE BELL

Description: Your bird hits the button in the center of a service bell to make the bell "ding."

Prerequisite: None.

Equipment: A service bell, the kind found on store counters and used to call for assistance. Attach a round piece of cardboard to the center ringer button, about 2 inches in diameter.

Instructions: Let your bird watch you hit the cardboard and make the service bell ding. Make it into a game. Hit it a few times and then offer it to your bird. Try to get him to touch it with his beak. See whether putting a dab of peanut butter on it will get him to touch it. Usually you can get him to make some sort of a

I'm ringing, is anybody there?

noise when touching it. P&R, and then you hit it again. Some birds will hit the table with their beaks when they are angry or upset. Use that moment to grab the bell and put it under their beak to get them to hit the bell instead of the table.

Cassie, my Caique, pounds the table with her beak when she is mad. I use the moment to grab the service bell, which I keep handy just for these occasions, and put in right under her beak. She then hits the piece of cardboard I have attached to the center button and makes it ding. I tap it with my finger, and then she hits it again. Usually she is so intrigued by causing the sound that she forgets what she was mad about. After your bird has gotten the idea of striking the cardboard, cut down the size of the cardboard, until it is barely larger than the bell's ringer button. Finally remove the cardboard altogether, and your bird should be able to zero in on the button at once. No physical cue is needed, and any verbal cue will do. The sight of the service bell is enough.

SKATING

Description: The bird climbs onto the skates and then maneuvers the skates to turn them and guide them with his feet to wherever you designate.

Prerequisite: None, but lots of treats and patience are required.

Equipment: Sturdy skates that won't break when dropped. You can make them yourself, but they are now readily available in bird catalogs, specialty bird magazines, and on the Internet. Most skates for birds are made of plastic. Skates must have guards on the outside of the wheels so the wheels will not catch on one another. The guards help the skates to slide past each other when your bird uses his natural pigeon-toed gait to skate forward. Some skates come with training rods. This is a good feature. Training rods are slender rods about a foot long that can be screwed into the front of bird skates to help you, the trainer, promote or control the forward motion of the skates. They are just meant to be used early in the learning process. After your bird understands what you want, the rods are not needed and should be removed. No verbal or physical cues are necessary to perform this trick; the skates become the cue.

Instructions: At first you want the skates to remain stationary. Use the training rods to keep the skates in place, or you can use double-sided tape to stick the wheels to the table. You can also place the skates on blocks so they don't touch the table and are, therefore, completely immobile.

One way to teach skating is by shaping the process to encourage your bird to move toward the skates and then rewarding him each time he goes near them. As your bird begins to understand that approaching the skates gets him a treat, encourage him to get closer and closer before P&R, until the bird must touch the skates to get his treat. Narrow your criteria more to make him touch them and eventually put his foot on a skate. This should be greatly rewarded and praised. With patience and repetition, your bird will begin climbing onto the skates. As he begins to understand that standing on the skates gets a reward, lengthen the amount of time he must remain in place to get his treat.

There is a faster way to teach this trick. If your bird is not afraid of the skates and if you can pick him up with your hands over his back, as was suggested in chapter 2, then just pick him up and place him on the skates and P&R. For milestones in the socialization of your bird, see the Tameness Scale discussion in chapter 2. Quietly hold him and praise him while he is standing on the skates until he is comfortable being there. Reward him while he is just standing on the skates. Let

Kiri on skates.

your bird realize that it is the standing on the skates that is being rewarded, and he must remain on the skates to get his treat. Then let him practice getting on and off the skates to get P&R.

Next, take the skates off the blocks or remove the tape from the wheels. This is where training rods help. Have your bird climb onto the skates as before but let them move a little as he does so. The training rods will help control this movement. Reward the bird for staying on the skates. Then move the skates forward by using the training rods, first in unison, then as the bird gets used to the motion, move the skates independently in a skating motion. The bird now knows he is being rewarded for staying on the skates and moving his feet with the skates. Try introducing a flat board that you have slanted just slightly to make it easy for him to move the skates forward.

With repetition and patience, and even some luring with a treat, your bird will begin to move the skates himself. When he does, reward him for any movement of the skates at all. Then start increasing the distance he must move the skates before being rewarded.

When he is mounting the skates by himself and skating the length of the training table, introduce the next variable. Now you want him to be able to steer the skates. Have him practice skating the length of the table, to the table perch, and getting off the skates and onto the perch, where you P&R. Next, when he has the idea of skating to the table perch, move the perch a little to one side so that to reach the perch he must turn the skates in that direction. With a little persistence and with you luring him with a treat, he will make the correction. Then keep increasing the amount your bird must turn. After he has mastered steering his skates, you can eventually ask him to turn a complete circle, first in one direction and then the other. Remember the *turn around* you taught as a beginning trick in chapter 5? Use the cue of an index finger making a small circle over your bird's head to signal him to turn around. Only when he can successfully steer his skates will he have mastered the art of skating.

RIDING A BICYCLE

Description: To complete this trick the bird must climb onto a bicycle and ride it the length of the training table. This is a trick for any size bird, but I have never seen a really small bicycle, so you are probably limited in teaching this trick by the size of the bicycle you can find.

Prerequisite: The bird should know at least some basic tricks before attempting this trick.

Equipment: The most difficult part of this trick is finding the bicycle. Bicycles are very hard to come by. They usually are made by hand and so are very expensive. Occasionally you will find one advertised on the Internet.

Instructions: Put the bicycle up on blocks so the wheels are not touching the table. The pedals should move freely. After first getting your bird used to seeing the bicycle so he accepts it as just another harmless prop, place your bird on the bicycle so that one foot is on each pedal. I find doing this is so much quicker then trying to shape the bird by little increments to finally touch the bicycle. Hold him with his feet on the pedals until he relaxes and is comfortable with it. Talk to him and praise him and as soon as you can remove your hands, reward him. I am

Where's your helmet?

assuming you have a bird who has been taught many other tricks and so placing him on the bicycle will not unduly alarm him. This is a more complicated trick so it should definitely not be taught until there is complete trust between you and your bird.

Usually a bird will automatically lean forward and grasp the handlebars with his beak for balance, but it doesn't really matter. He will be balancing mainly on the pedals. Usually a bird, in shifting his weight, will press down on one pedal or the other, and the opposite pedal will then move up causing the bird to have to shift his weight again. Each time the bird makes the pedals move be sure to P&R. Do not let him get off the bicycle. You can P&R while he remains in place. Soon your bird will figure out that to get his treat all he has to do is to make the pedals move. Very soon he will be pedaling up and down easily since the bike is on blocks and not touching the table.

Next coax your bird to get off the bicycle by holding a treat so that he has to get off the bike to get it. Then help him to get back on the bike. Soon he should be able to do this on his own and then push the pedals freely. When he can do this readily, take the bicycle off the blocks and help him mount the bicycle by holding it steady for him. Now when he pushes down on the pedals he will be met with some resistance, and the bike will move forward. Keep up a steady stream of encouragement. You do not want him to get off the bicycle. Hold the bicycle steady at first and just control the forward movement until he is not startled by it. Usually at this time your bird will decide to grab the handlebars for balance if he has not done so before. Let your bird slowly take control of pushing on the pedals. Training wheels will keep the bike in the upright position, and after your bird starts pedaling to your excited and delighted praise, you are almost there.

Start requiring your bird to pedal a little farther each time before rewarding him, but use your voice to continue encouraging him. Finally stop the bike and ask your bird to dismount; then jackpot him, give him a huge reward! The final piece to train is to have your bird mount the bike on his own, ride the length of the training table, and then dismount and come to you. When your bird can do all this, you are in the upper echelon of bird trainers!

Chapter 10

Innovative Tricks

Innovative tricks refer to behaviors or perhaps antics that your bird performs spontaneously. Some of these behaviors are priceless, and when turned into cued tricks can become the most outstanding tricks in your bird's repertoire. What does your bird now do spontaneously that you would like to "capture" and make into a cued trick? Tail flicking, shaking or fanning his feathers, throwing objects like balls or other props, verbalizations, and talking are all natural behaviors exhibited by some birds that can be captured and given a cue. Watch your bird and see what he offers. You'll be surprised at what you see.

A specific example for me would be my Caique's ability to hop. Only certain parrots can hop, and if you have a species that does not hop, there is no way you can teach him to do so. But if your bird is of a species that does hop naturally (certain Cockatoos, Lories, Cockatiels, Caiques, and probably others), then you can capture this behavior by giving it a verbal and/or physical cue and rewarding your bird each time he performs the behavior. For innovative tricks, you need lots of patience. It might be awhile before your bird repeats a particular behavior again, but be ready when he does with lots of praise and reward (P&R). After your parrot learns that a repeat of a particular behavior earns him a reward, he will start to repeat it more often, until you can bring the behavior under the control of a cue. Now it is a bona fide trick.

I will give you examples of how I connect some of my birds' spontaneous behaviors with cues, and perhaps it will give you ideas how you might be able to do the same thing with your birds.

HOPPING

I will start with Cassie's, my Caique's spontaneous hopping behavior mentioned at the beginning of this chapter. Since she hopped a lot, it was just a matter of figuring out what triggered the behavior. I had seen a trainer who had a Cockatoo who hopped on cue, so I asked him how he captured the behavior. He said, "Oh that was easy. I just slapped the table and she would hop." I thought, "Now that doesn't sound too difficult," so my next training session with Cassie, I slapped the table! Well, Cassie was really startled. She took off from the table fast, scared to death, and ran and hid under a chair. So it was back to the drawing board for me.

I was teaching her colors with the *ring on the peg* trick (see Chapter 7, "Simple Tricks Based on the Retrieve"), and I noticed she often picked up the blue ring and hopped around with it a bit. I have no idea why, whether she was mad at it, or pleased with herself, or what. She no longer does it, but at the time she did it just often enough for me to quickly give her a physical cue of my fist on the table in front of her. I would say, "hop, hop" and then, of course, laugh delightedly and P&R. Sometimes it seems you can't help but use *constructs;* that is, attributing human traits to things that parrots do, even though we really have no idea why they are doing it. But Cassie did seem to look at me incredulously as though to say, "You want me to do *what?*" Finally she gave a tentative hop, and I practically hugged her. From then on I worked with her to increase the number of hops she performed, whether in place, or to hop to a particular place as when she hops with the ball to place it in the basket.

What I learned from this was to just be patient. Watch your bird, see what he offers, and be quick with the P&R. You'll be surprised at what you see. Remember, your bird is doing what for him is a natural behavior, and he will not in the beginning understand what he's being rewarded for. Innovative tricks can sometimes take a lot of time to teach, but once captured with a cue can be a lot of fun.

An innovative behavior, hopping, becomes a cued trick for Cassie.

SCRATCHING HEAD

I noticed Squawk, my Blue-crowned Conure, scratched her head fairly often, and the position she took to do so was really quite cute. I decided to see whether I could put that behavior on cue. Every time she was on the training stand and scratched her head, I would quickly put up my hand in an awkward position and scratch my head also. I am sure Squawk was giving me some very strange looks, but she quickly got the idea, since she got a big treat every time she did it, and soon she would lift her leg to scratch her head every time she saw me raise my hand in this peculiar way, to scratch my head. From this developed the idea of the salute where I

Another innovative trick: Squawk scratching her head on cue.

would just bring my hand to my forehead and she would also not then do a head scratch but just lift her leg to touch her head.

PLACING OBJECT UNDER WING

I noticed Squawk wrapped one wing around a small bell that was hanging on a cord suspended above her cage. I have no idea why she did this. It's something she still does quite frequently. But I decided it was an interesting behavior that I would try to capture. I got a similar bell and cord and brought them to the training table. I let her examine them and try to ring the tiny bell. Then I gently placed the bell under the same wing I had observed her using. She allowed me to do so, and then quickly consumed the proffered treats. This trick did not take long to teach as I did not have to wait for her to offer the behavior. Also you must remember Squawk is a pretty well-trained bird so she catches on to tricks very quickly. Soon she was opening her wing to take the bell. Next I had her take a few steps, keeping the bell under her wing, and finally carry the bell a short ways and then hand it to me. It was but a short step from that to accepting different objects to place under her wing. First it was a small purse also attached to a cord that she could take with her when she wanted to go "shopping." Now I can just hand her an object to place under her wing.

The way I am now using this trick is in a chain of tricks I describe in the next chapter on chaining. In the chain of tricks she has "rescued" a baby bird that has fallen into the well and she decides to protect it by "taking it under her wing."

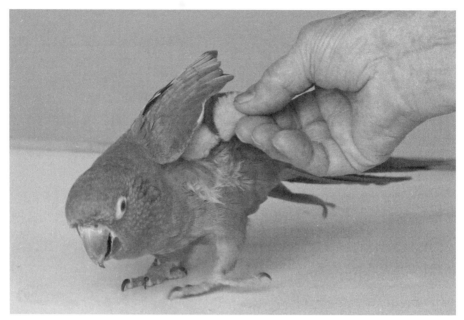

Squawk takes a baby bird under her wing.

PUTTING FOOT TO BEAK

This is a behavior I noticed Poopsie, my Green-cheeked Conure, doing when I was teaching her to *play dead* (see chapter 9, "Miscellaneous Tricks"). Sometimes when I would touch her tail while helping her to lie on her back, she would put her foot in her mouth. I don't know why or what it meant to her. But I rewarded her when she would do so. Eventually while she was sitting on the table perch, I touched her tail and right away her foot went to her beak. Bingo, I had a new trick. Now, how could I use it? My solution: I had her put a "baby" to bed in its cradle, cover it and rock the cradle. Then when she was back on the table stand I asked her what the baby was doing. My one hand was already on the table behind her so it was very easy to just barely touch her tail and she would immediately put her foot to her beak. I would say, "Oh, the baby was sucking its thumb!"

DANCING, BOBBING, AND WEAVING

Most parrots will bob and weave at one time or another while sitting on a perch. One way to elicit this behavior is for you to dance around and bob and weave in front of your bird, and sing and act excited. Often the bird will pick up on your mood and start to weave, too. Sometimes it is certain music you can play that will start your bird "dancing." Then it is just a matter of giving a physical and/or verbal cue when he starts the behavior and giving lots of P&R. Pretty soon your bird will respond to your cues with this behavior. Your bird will be delighted when you join him in a bit of craziness.

STRETCHING

Another example of a spontaneous performance of a behavior that almost all parrots do and that you might be interested in putting under the control of a cue is stretching. Many parrots enjoy stretching their wings frequently, and then sometimes follow that by stretching out their legs. When you reward this spontaneous behavior and bring it under the control of a cue, it becomes a trick behavior. Use your imagination as to what you want to do with the trick. It could be a warm-up exercise before skating or riding a bicycle.

A Macaw performs some innovative dance steps.

NODDING HEAD YES

My Blue and Gold Macaw, Charlie, was a rescue bird who hadn't been handled much, and because he was not well socialized, I did not want to start with my normal beginning tricks of *wave, turn around,* and *shake hands* (see chapter 5, "Tricks That Don't Require Props"). At first he did not like to be touched, but I noticed when he was on a stand, he occasionally bobbed his head. So I started with that and used a "thumbs up" for a physical cue and an enthusiastic "yes, yes" verbal cue. I followed up with plenty of P&R. That became his first trick. It's not something I would normally recommend, but keep alert with your bird and see what he offers that you can capitalize on. You can almost feel what he must be thinking, "I do this motion and this crazy woman here gets all excited and feeds me an almond. I'll humor her and do it again and see whether I can get her to give me another almond." I know, another construct, but it does seem to fit.

SHAKING HEAD NO

This behavior I treated the same as *nodding head yes.* Every time your bird shakes his head or sways from side to side, quick give him a cue and P&R. I used the physical cue of shaking a finger back and forth in front of Charlie, as you might do if you were saying "no, no, no." But I did not use a verbal cue like "no" for this trick as I did not want to use the word "no" in a trick behavior when giving a reward. I reserve "no," usually strongly said, for those few emergencies when you need to stop an action at once, and you need a strong invective to get attention. It works for me.

RAISING THE RUFF OR NECK FEATHERS

This trick is one Zena, my Hawk-headed Parrot, can perform; you could also probably apply it to birds like Cockatoos who can raise their head feathers, or crests. I noticed Zena would raise her exotic ruff, or the circle of feathers around her neck, when she was excited or agitated. I would cue her with a flick of my fingers in front of her face. At first the flicking fingers in her face would alarm her and cause her to raise her ruff, but after awhile she got used to the motion, and it didn't bother her so much. I then found that I could put the fingers of my free hand behind her neck and actually physically manipulate her feathers and cause them to rise. Along with much P&R, she got the connection and finally would raise the ruff on the original cue of the flicking fingers, which I then retired to a small signal farther away. For you Cockatoo or Cockatiel owners, you might try the same to get your bird to raise his crest in response to a cue.

Chapter 11

Chaining Tricks

Chaining tricks is one of my favorite subjects and is my specialty. Individual tricks are great to teach, but when you can put tricks together to tell a story, it is so much more interesting. *Chaining* is having your bird perform one trick after another, often while you are narrating what he is doing so that it tells a story. For instance your bird puts a ball into a basket. Well, that is fine, so what next? What can you do with that trick to make it more interesting? Now visualize this chain of tricks: You toss a ball onto the table, your bird picks it up, and starts toward the basket holding it. He then does a 360-degree turn *(turn around)*. Then he proceeds to dribble the ball down the court, maybe even doing a *roll over* while still holding the ball, and finally he dunks the ball in the basket. Which scenario is the more interesting? The individual tricks are not all that difficult, but chained together they become sensational. My whole show now is almost completely chained tricks because they are so much more spectacular. After your bird has learned a particular chain of tricks, he usually has to be started on the first one only, and he will do the rest of the tricks in order without further direction. You praise and reward him only when he has finished the completed set.

Chaining is not that difficult to teach. Start with teaching individual tricks. Teach many tricks, as many as you like. The more tricks your bird learns, the more quickly he will learn each succeeding trick. As your bird learns various tricks, you will start thinking of ways to combine them.

PUTTING IT ALL TOGETHER

I will start with the longest and most complicated chain I do to show you how it was put together. I have Squawk, my Blue-crowned Conure, take a quarter from me and go to a toy cash register to get change. The chain ends twelve tricks later with Squawk putting a baby bird from a buggy into a cradle and then rocking the baby to sleep. Intrigued? This is how I put it all together. Remember, each of these tricks was trained separately before being chained into one long, exciting sequence.

You taught your bird to *turn a crank* in chapter 8, "Advanced Tricks Based on the Retrieve," and graduated from that to turning a crank on a toy cash register. So now he can turn the crank, which opens the cash register, but what will you have him do after that? You can give him a quarter and ask for change. He will take the quarter from you, and then you indicate he is to put the quarter on top of the cash register drawer. All this is explained in chapter 6, "Teaching the Basic Retrieve Command." Your bird will go to the cash register, leave the quarter where indicated, turn the crank, and open the register. Now he will find a dime in the drawer. You will signal him to bring you the dime with the open hand *bring it to me* cue taught in chapter 6. You have now put four individual tricks together. Go through this chain many times, encouraging with your voice and maybe hand cues to guide him to the next step. Give your bird a food reward only when he has completed the entire chain. Your voice is telling him to keep going, that he is not done yet. Pretty soon all you have to do is hand him the quarter and with the appropriate prop available, he will complete the chain quite quickly all by himself. Then he deserves a big praise and reward (P&R).

Now, what can you add? He brings you the dime and what do you want to do with it? You could have him put it in a piggy bank, give it to someone, buy some groceries that he could then put into a grocery cart, which you could then develop into an interesting skit. Or maybe he could put the quarter into a slot machine, depending on what props you have available. The following paragraphs explain the chain of tricks I put together.

Your bird has probably by now learned how to pull a basket up to a perch, one of the easier tricks taught in chapter 9, "Miscellaneous Tricks." My perch is on a well, and I declared my well to be a wishing well, which required a coin to be put in before a wish would be granted. So I had my bird deposit his dime in the well. Just like you did back in teaching the *retrieve,* you can do this by tapping on the well, indicating where your bird is to put the dime. P&R each little step now. Next you want him to climb a ladder to the top of the well. You taught him to climb ladders way back in the beginning, so show him the ladder you want him to climb and indicate by tapping the top where you want him to climb to. Again, be sure to P&R each step. If he isn't sure or if you haven't taught him any of these individual tricks, work on each trick separately before trying to chain them into this skit.

Your bird is now at the top of the ladder and standing on the crosspiece of the wishing well. He sees the basket with his treat in it hanging there, and since he knows this trick well, he should immediately begin to pull it up. Just give him praise at this point as his treat is in the basket.

You now have several more parts to your chain:

1. Your bird takes a quarter and places it on cash register.
2. He opens register and gets a dime.
3. He takes dime to the well and puts it in.
4. He climbs a ladder.
5. He pulls up a basket to get his reward.

You have chained five separate tricks! You can stop there, and you have a nice little scenario. But if you want to add more . . .

How about if a baby bird had fallen into the well, and your bird was asked to rescue it? That changes things a bit. Instead of getting a treat when he pulls up the basket he finds a baby bird in it. You have to teach that as a separate trick. Go back to the training table and have your bird bring you a chick/baby bird from a basket similar to the one you are using on the well. Use your imagination as to what

constitutes a baby bird. I use one of those little yellow chicks you sometimes find in Easter egg baskets. A fluffy pompom with eyes or a felt creation could also pass as a baby bird or chick. Reward him each time he brings you the chick. He will soon get the idea that bringing you the chick is what gets him the reward. Then you are ready to proceed having him pull the baby up in the basket, take the baby out, and hand it to you to get his treat. This is breaking things down into small steps to gain your final goal.

Now your bird must hang onto the baby and turn around on top of the crosspiece before handing it to you. For some reason this was very

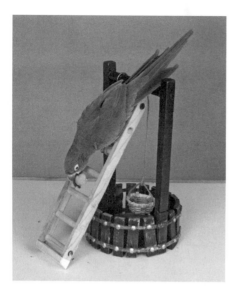

difficult for my bird to do and took many repetitions and much encouragement, even though she knew the *turn around* very well. So I went back to the training perch, to an earlier training stage, and had her do many *turn arounds,* this time holding the chick. Only when she was comfortable doing this did I return her to the well.

My bird also had difficulty climbing down the ladder holding onto the chick. So we worked on that part separately from the chain of tricks. But this is what chaining is. Even though you think your bird knows a particular trick, like going down a ladder head first, when you decide to add a small variation, like carrying something in her beak while going down the ladder, sometimes you have to go back and do some additional training. Don't be afraid to go back and retrain a trick or add to it. You can do that part separately while working on other parts of the chain or other tricks. Keep the lesson moving so your bird doesn't get bored with too much repetition of a particular part. You can always come back to a difficult part and work on it separately.

STILL MORE . . .

Are you still with me? You can stop at any point and have a nicely chained trick. As I said earlier, this has been my longest chained trick and the most complicated I do. But this wasn't the end; I'll go on with the rest of the chain in case you are still interested.

Your bird should give you the chick at the bottom of the ladder. Tell your bird everyone wants to know whether the baby is okay. He must ring the bell and let everyone know. You have previously taught him how to ring a bell so now he sees the bell prop and goes to the bell and rings it, a trick described in chapter 7, "Simple Tricks Based on the Retrieve."

I then ask my bird, Squawk, if she would like to take the baby under her wing. This is an innovative trick that Squawk does. I described it in chapter 10, "Innovative Tricks," but if your bird doesn't do that, you can instead suggest to your bird that he take the baby for a ride in his buggy. You have taught your bird to push things so teaching him now separately to push a baby buggy should not be a big reach. Also work with him on taking the chick from you and putting it in the buggy. These are all tricks based on the *retrieve* taught in chapter 6. Then combine these tricks: Your bird takes the chick from you, places it in the buggy, and pushes the buggy to wherever you des-

ignate. See, it's not so hard. This chain of tricks is all based on behaviors you taught earlier, combined to tell a story.

FINAL TOUCHES

If you have stayed with me this long, now add some final touches. Work with your bird on learning to steer the buggy. This is harder than it looks. Birds can usually push something straight ahead, but learning to turn it, too, is something else. Have your bird first try to just turn the buggy slightly toward your hand that will be holding a treat. Encourage him to turn it just a little more each time. Helping him to place his beak to the outside of the handle of the buggy will make turning easier. This step may take a while to perfect, but you can keep working on it while practicing other parts of the chain.

Next, have your bird push the buggy to a cradle with your *bring it to me* cue indicating the cradle. Soon this part will become easy, and he will automatically push the buggy to wherever he sees the cradle. Then using your *retrieve* cues, have him take the baby from the buggy and place it in the cradle. These are all in essence separate tricks and should be taught as such. Only when each part is learned can it be added to the chain. This is not something that can be taught overnight. Work away at it, bit by bit, until each part can be added to the whole.

The baby is now in the cradle. Ask your bird to cover the baby. I keep a small piece of cloth as a blanket in the bottom of the buggy. Your bird now takes this blanket from the buggy and puts it into the cradle. Since the baby is already in the cradle, it automatically gets covered. All the bird is doing is responding to his *retrieve* training and moving something from one place to another. Again, you should teach this separately. Finally you ask him to rock the cradle. I taught this by asking my bird to "step up" onto the cradle and then stopping him before he could put any weight on it, so he was just touching the cradle with his foot. This is much like you taught him to *shake hands*—to just touch your hand with his foot but not transfer any weight. Inevitably the cradle moves so it gives the illusion he is rocking the cradle.

Now, how's that for a long chain? Even if you stop at any part, you will still have a nice sequence. My own bird has gone through this chain enough times now that she knows the routine and so will proceed right to the end. If your bird bogs down, repeat a segment he can do successfully and P&R him for that.

I couldn't let things be; I have now added a battery-operated lamp that has a lever my bird has to step on to "turn out the light" after rocking the baby to sleep. See what those creative juices can produce? I count about thirteen tricks in this chain. Of course some of the tricks are duplicated, such as taking the quarter and putting it on the cash register, picking up the dime and putting it in the well, taking the baby and putting it into the buggy, and again taking the baby from the buggy and putting it into the cradle. All are similar *retrieve* tricks of taking an object from one place and putting it elsewhere. But with different props, it makes each trick look different. I think you can see why I have emphasized all along a good foundation in the *retrieve*. Now all of these derived tricks will be learned quite easily.

If you decide to do the entire chain, or even part of it, make a list of the individual tricks you will use and teach each one separately first. Only when he can do each trick alone should you put them all together. Of course, this is true for all the tricks you chain.

CHAINS OF TRICKS

That was just one long example to show you what you could do with your individual tricks. Here are some shorter chains starting with two trick chains and ending with ones that are a little more complicated. Don't apply any pressure on your bird. Chains work only when your bird runs through them happily. Always give extra P&R when a chain is complete. Never punish for a wrong move. Set your bird up for success by making it easy for him to do the right thing so he can always be rewarded. Remember, tricks are supposed to be fun. It is up to you to make it so.

Putting a Lei on a Doll

1. Your bird places a lei on a doll.
2. He then gives the doll a kiss.

Recycling

1. Your bird places different objects into their correspondingly labeled containers: GLASS, PLASTIC, PAPER, CANS, and so on.

2. Have your bird repeat the task with you calling out by name which object he is to pick up first, second, and so on.

Playing Baseball

1. Your bird holds a bat in his beak and shakes his head "no," thus hitting a ball on a stand.
2. He runs the three bases.
3. Told to steal home, your bird runs to home plate and picks up the stand the ball was originally on and brings it to the trainer.

Bowling

1. Your bird picks a ball up from a receptacle and places it at the top of a bowling lane.

2. He then pushes the ball with his beak down the lane and into the pins.

3. He walks to the pins and knocks down any left standing.

Doing a Fireman Act

1. Your bird climbs a long ladder to the top.

2. He then slides down the adjacent pole.

3. He picks up a fireman's hat and places it on a rack.

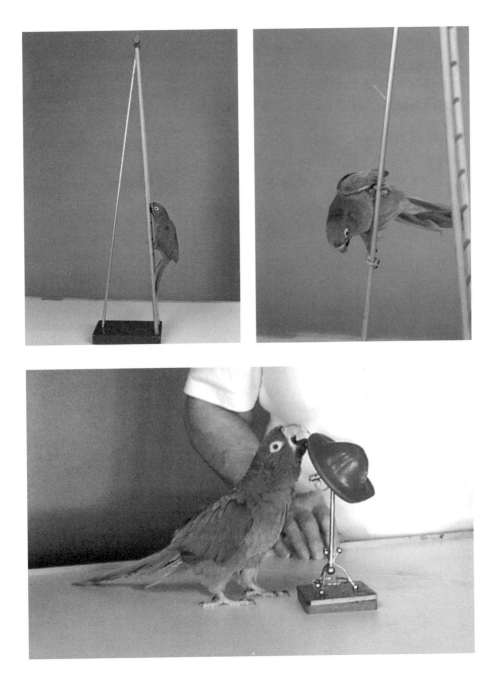

Getting Shot

1. While sitting on a "perch" you are holding, your bird falls over backward when shot, by pointing a finger at him and saying "bang," or by using a toy gun.

2. Your bird remains hanging upside down from a perch and when held over an object on the table, such as a flag, banner, or whatever, picks it up to display it, while suspended upside down.

3. He rights himself when instructed to do so.

Playing Soccer

1. Your bird pushes a lawn mower around the playing field and eventually out through the goal posts to first "mow the lawn."

2. He then pushes a soccer ball with his beak down the field, around fake bird interceptors, to end up pushing the ball through the goal posts.

3. He finally climbs to the top of the goal posts and takes a bow or does a *big eagle* to show he has just scored a goal.

Taking Out the Trash

1. Your bird steps on a trash can to open the lid.
2. He picks up pieces of paper, small tin cans, and so on and places them into the can.
3. He closes the lid of the can.

Shopping for Groceries

1. Your bird pushes a grocery cart to some grocery shelves.

2. He takes groceries off the shelves and places them in the cart.

3. He rings a service bell to call the grocer.

4. He places a "credit card" in a slot to pay for the groceries.

5. He pushes the grocery cart back to where he started.

Setting a Table

1. Your bird opens cupboard doors to show the dishes inside.

2. He puts the dishes on the table.

3. He then puts the dishes back into the cupboard.

4. He closes the cupboard doors.

Climbing a Cuckoo Clock

1. Your bird climbs up into a cuckoo clock.

2. He opens the door and steps out onto a platform as though he is a cuckoo bird.

3. He rings a hand bell three times to let all the children know it is time for school to get out.

4. He puts the hand bell down and backs into the clock.

5. He climbs down the ladder and out of the clock back to the tabletop.

Playing Music and Dancing

1. Your bird touches various keys on a keyboard.

2. He ends by pressing a key to make the music continuous.

3. He climbs onto a table perch and bobs and sways to the music.

4. He lifts each foot alternating feet, several times, and then he does pirouettes *(turn arounds)* turning in each direction.

5. He ends by taking a bow.

Going to the Mailbox

1. Your bird lowers a flag on the mailbox.

2. He opens the door to the mailbox.

3. He removes the mail and brings it to the trainer.

4. He takes a letter from trainer and places the letter into the mailbox.

5. He closes the mailbox.

6. He raises the flag on the mailbox.

Making a Parrot Cocktail

1. Your bird climbs onto a coffee mug and pretends to take a drink from it.

2. He hops off and does a dead bird act.

3. He allows himself to be picked up while on his back and placed on top of a cocktail glass.

4. He holds a pretend olive in his feet to make a "martini."

5. He stays on the glass as the glass is picked up and held up for a "toast."

6. He allows the olive to be removed and then grasps the trainer's fingers to be lifted from the glass and returned to the table perch.

Doing a Gymnastics Routine on the Uneven Bars

1. Your bird climbs onto the low bar and does two-foot rolls facing out (to your right).

2. He turns around and faces the high bar.

3. He jumps to the high bar.

4. He does two-foot rolls on the high bar facing the other way (to your left).

5. He turns around to face the low bar again and jumps to it.

6. He does a one-foot roll on the low bar, facing right.

7. He does a half *turn around* to face left and then does a back flip dismount.

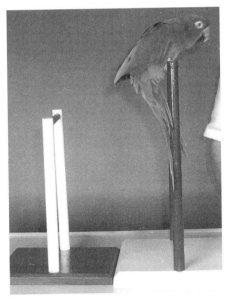

These are just a few of the possibilities for chaining tricks, putting them together in fun ways. You can come up with chains and accompanying story lines from current events, well-known locations, sports, professions, fables or folk tales, themes like a Western saga or just funny commentary on what your bird is doing. Let your creative juices flow and you will be surprised at what you can come up with!

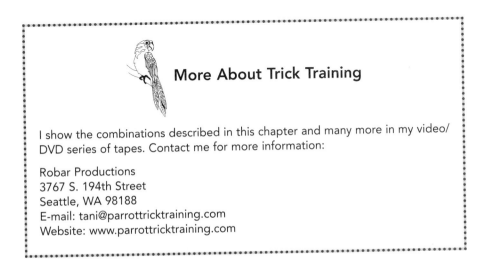

More About Trick Training

I show the combinations described in this chapter and many more in my video/DVD series of tapes. Contact me for more information:

Robar Productions
3767 S. 194th Street
Seattle, WA 98188
E-mail: tani@parrottricktraining.com
Website: www.parrottricktraining.com

Chapter 12

Verbalizations and Talking

Your talking parrot can learn to say some things with understanding. Even your nontalking parrot can understand and respond to what you say. How you interact with a talking bird and what you say to him are important. Many talking birds are able to name people and pets in their household, ask for food when they want it, and call for other pets in the household. Parrots have learned entire answering machine messages and one-sided phone conversations. Your parrot can also be trained to respond to verbal cues so he speaks on command.

Parrots do not only "parrot" what they hear; your parrot can vocalize with comprehension. You'll learn how to guide his learning in this chapter. You'll need to decide what level of learning you want for your parrot and what level of commitment you are willing to make to his vocalizations. It's helpful to think about why you want a talking parrot. Consider whether you want your parrot to say things indiscriminately—to parrot a few cute phrases—or whether you want to establish some communication with your parrot. Perhaps you want to show off to friends and have your parrot say words and phrases on cue. You might even want to train parrots professionally or put on shows in your community.

Although it does happen that a parrot will blurt out a word clearly after only hearing it once, it is more likely that your parrot will go through stages of learning to speak. You will notice your parrot mumbling or whistling first, using the intonations you use in speech. Your parrot might even use quiet times during the day or just before sleeping to review his vocabulary and practice vocalizations. Over time, your parrot's mumbling will get clearer. Reward those first attempts at vocalizations and keep talking to your parrot and responding to him when he vocalizes. As your parrot starts to say some things, you can ask him to say them more clearly for you.

YOU ARE ALREADY TRAINING YOUR PARROT

The major motivation for a parrot to vocalize is to have his needs met. Parrots are self-centered pets, and they do things that please them and help them acquire food, company, and entertainment. You may have already been teaching your verbal birds some things. When your parrot screams, do you run to him? That is a reward for your parrot. He loves your company and looks for ways to have more of it.

This Lilac-crowned Amazon is listening to and repeating what family members say, whether they train her or not.

Your parrot has probably noticed that you run to answer the phone, microwave, or kitchen timer. This is not lost on an intelligent parrot. When he wants you to run to him, he imitates what looks like the obvious flock call to assemble the flock, he imitates the phone, the microwave, or the timer. Parrots hear and vocalize at frequencies we aren't capable of hearing as human beings. Their vocal equipment is more sophisticated than our lowly voice boxes, too. Parrots can make the equivalent of two sounds at once, so they can manage electronic beeps and tones we can't imagine duplicating.

You can use this knowledge to guide your bird's learning experience. Make sure he gets what he wants when he is learning vocalizations you want. And make sure to react with *enthusiasm* when he says a word you want him to say.

Any parrot species can theoretically learn to talk, and conversely, no species of parrot can be guaranteed to talk. Some species speak more clearly and readily than others. Unless you are adopting an older bird who is already talking, be aware that many birds do not talk. Don't set yourself up for disappointment if you are purchasing a baby parrot in the expectation that he will become a good talker. He could be a nontalking bird. Each bird has his own wonderful personality and can become a good pet regardless of whether he ever talks.

TRAINING YOUR PARROT TO TALK

You probably can't help but teach your bird to talk if he is a vocal bird and is one of the species who learns to talk readily. When your parrot says a word you would like him to repeat, praise him and offer him a treat. Make it a big deal. Your

The morning and evening are good times to give parrots talking lessons, as John Vincent is doing here with a Double Yellow-headed Amazon.

parrot learns words said with emotion and enthusiasm. If there's a word you want your parrot to say, say it to him with enthusiasm. Play with the word. Sing the word. Make the word enticing. Say it just as emphatically as any four-letter word you might say when you hit your thumb with a hammer. That'll get your parrot's attention.

Parrots vocalize naturally in the morning and evening, so if you can, plan to train your bird during those times. Because your feedback is important to your bird, you're never really *not* training him, anyway. Your parrot will be picking up sounds and trying them out whether you're teaching them to him deliberately or not.

At first, you'll be rewarding your parrot for an attempt to say something. Anything! If your parrot mumbles, chirps, or tweets, and there's some chance he's trying to say what you want him to say, reward him for it. Say the word you think he is saying, or something you want him to say. If he's asking for something like a treat or a shower, react as though he said the word clearly and then say the word or request yourself. Over time the word will become more distinct. When you know your parrot is trying to say a certain word, and he's been saying it for awhile, you can insist that he speak clearly before praising and rewarding him.

Sometimes parrots are enchanted with our speech or singing and start learning whole phrases. When a parrot is just learning to talk, that attempt often sounds like mumbling, or sounds with the intonation of human speech but without distinct words being spoken. Often your parrot will start saying a phrase. You can encourage him by reacting appropriately to what he is trying to say or by repeating the phrase for him.

ONCE MORE, WITH MEANING

When a parrot merely "parrots" a phrase he doesn't associate any meaning to it. He is vocalizing and only knows that it brings him your attention or another reward. You can teach your parrot to say phrases in a meaningful way by teaching him what your vocalizations mean. When you come in and out of a room, say "hello" and "good-bye." When you put your parrot to bed, say "nighty night." Ask your bird whether he wants a shower, and then take him into the shower with you, or bring out the spray bottle to give him one. Name the foods you give your parrot. Remember that a parrot remembers words said with enthusiasm, so spend some time saying "apple" in many tones. "What a nice apple, yum!" and take a nibble yourself. If you teach your parrot words the way you would teach a child or someone just learning the language, you should get results.

TALKING BACK

Your parrot will best learn to associate words with their meanings when he gets feedback for his efforts. A number of recorded devices are designed to repeat a phrase over and over for your parrot while you're out of the house. Not surprisingly,

Your bird will learn to talk better from you than from a talking device.

this does not work. The recording has no meaning for your parrot and doesn't produce food or socialization. It is repetitious and boring to our social, bright-feathered companions. They soon learn to ignore it. Parrots are social creatures, and it is the interaction between you and your parrot that will help him to learn. You could use a recording as an aid, if you and your parrot both listen to a tape or a recording together, and you respond to it. Respond to it by enjoying the recording with exclamations, by repeating some of the words, and by using the words in different ways. You could reinforce the pronunciation of a new word by leaving a recording of your own voice occasionally. Unless you also use the words said on a tape, it is not likely your parrot will learn from a recording alone, but it can be an aid to his speech education.

THE MODEL/RIVAL METHOD

Dr. Irene Pepperberg has been doing intelligence studies with Alex the African Grey since 1981. Prior to Dr. Pepperberg's work with parrots, it was not thought in the scientific community that parrots were intelligent beings. Their brain is structured differently. It really was believed they merely "parroted" words without distinguishing meaning for them. But Dr. Pepperberg and Alex have shown that parrots score as high as chimpanzees and dolphins on some intelligence tests. Alex can name objects, matter, shapes, and colors, specify same and different, and can even throw a tantrum when he is upset by naming every color or shape but the right one!

Dr. Pepperberg achieved success with Alex by developing the Model/Rival Method of teaching him. In addition, she made rewards meaningful. Instead of working for peanuts, literally, Alex got to touch and mouth the object he was naming. Or he could ask for a treat instead. This is in contrast to previous parrot

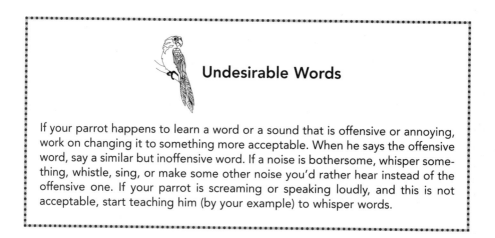

Undesirable Words

If your parrot happens to learn a word or a sound that is offensive or annoying, work on changing it to something more acceptable. When he says the offensive word, say a similar but inoffensive word. If a noise is bothersome, whisper something, whistle, sing, or make some other noise you'd rather hear instead of the offensive one. If your parrot is screaming or speaking loudly, and this is not acceptable, start teaching him (by your example) to whisper words.

In the Model/Rival Method, the trainer and a person who models behavior and is a rival for the parrot's attention work together. Here Diane Grindol and Tom Roudybush work with Popeye the Grey.

research, in which a parrot was rewarded with food that had nothing to do with a word or phrase being taught.

In the Model/Rival Method, Alex and two people are present. At first, the two people have a conversation about an object. "What's this?" asks a person acting as the trainer. The other person, acting as the parrot, is both the *model* for Alex's behavior and his *rival* for the trainer's attention and reward. The Model/Rival responds "paper." The first person responds "yes," with enthusiasm and offers praise and a reward, or she could say "say better" or even "no" if the answer is incorrect. If the answer is incorrect, she then turns her back on the Model/Rival person. Then the first person still acting as the trainer asks Alex the same thing she was just asking the Model/Rival person.

It turns out that the social interaction between the trainer and the parrot are important to parrot learning. With the help of another person, you can use this technique at home. Just don't expect results on a par with Alex the African Grey. Alex has had constant attention and hours of training daily. Dr. Pepperberg has had the help of graduate students and volunteers.

If you have someone to help you, you can use the Model/Rival Method to help your parrot name things or identify colors. You can also use it, quite practically, to teach desirable behaviors. You can use it to help familiarize your parrot with a new toy or to teach him to eat a new food.

In the Model/Rival Method, the parrot receives a reward for the object he has named.

THE POSITIVE REWARD METHOD

I use two different methods to teach a parrot who is already talking to talk on cue. If your parrot says a word or a phrase you like, repeat the word as soon as he says it and praise and reward (P&R). Do that a few times and then say the word first and see whether he will say it after you. Quite often your bird will then repeat it after you. Make a game of it and get him to repeat the word until he is doing it readily right after you. Then add your cue word, words, or even a question. Say your cue words first and then the word you want him to repeat immediately after and let him then say his word. Pair the two continuously for a time until your bird gets the connection and starts anticipating you by giving the correct response as soon as you ask the question. Then give lots of P&R.

For example, start with a word your bird already says, like "hello." When you hear him say "hello," you say "hello," too. When he is saying the word often because he enjoys the interaction with you, then you try saying the word first to see whether he will repeat it after you this time. Often he will, and then you can delightedly P&R. Say the word again and see whether he will repeat it after you. If he does, P&R and keep doing it. If he offers the word on his own, ignore it and do not P&R. P&R only when he repeats the word after you. When he is consistently doing that, then start adding what will be your cue word or words. "What do you say when you answer the telephone? Hello." Your parrot should then say "hello," too. Keep saying the cue words, emphasizing *telephone* and then say "hello," after which your bird should also say "hello." P&R. Repeat this combination often enough, and it won't be long before your bird will anticipate when to say "hello," and not wait for you to say it first. He will respond to the word "telephone" with "hello," giving you a cued question and response.

If your bird is not already saying a word you want to use, then you have to start from the beginning and teach him a new word to add to this question and response game. Say the word you want your bird to say, repeatedly and with enthusiasm as described before, until your bird will repeat it reliably after you. Then change to the format described previously and add the cue word before you say the word he is now repeating after you. For example, you want your bird to be able to say his name. Your bird's name is Charlie, so you keep saying "Charlie" to him until he says it after you. Then you add the cue word "name." It doesn't matter how you word the question, as long as you finish with the word "name." You could say: "Tell us your name," or "What is your name?," or even "Do you have a name?" "Name" is the important word and what he will respond to. So ask your question, saying "name" loud and clear, and follow that with "Charlie," a word he now knows. When he says Charlie after you, of course P&R. Do the combination enough times, and he will start anticipating you. When he hears the word "name," he will respond "Charlie."

The more you work with your bird on this type of cue and response, the easier it will become for your bird to understand what you want and respond appropriately. Don't reward him if he responds too quickly and doesn't wait for your full question, however. I used to have that trouble with Squawk, my Blue-crowned Conure. She had been taught to say "pretty bird" early on as I was told that those were easy words for a bird to learn and say. Then I wanted to add a question and put the response on cue, so I would ask her, "Are you an ugly bird or a pretty bird?" thinking that my saying "pretty bird" as part of the question would trigger her response of "pretty bird." Instead, after getting the combination, she would never wait for the full question and as soon as I asked the first part of the question "Are you an ugly bird or . . ." she would cut me short and answer "pretty bird" without letting me finish the question. I covered by telling her with mock irritation, "Hey, wait for the cue!" and not rewarding her. But her answer always made the audience laugh, so I gave up and decided to do it her way, and from then on rewarded her for the interruption and quick response, only pretending to be annoyed. I made it a part of the show. I learned quickly not to make the response word also a part of the cue.

EXPECTATIONS

Even if you have a very intelligent parrot who responds to you with understanding and who knows how to ask for what he wants, the level of conversation you will have with your feathered friend does not equal that of an intelligent person. You won't be talking to each other in complex sentences, and you won't be discussing philosophy. You will be communicating, however!

Chapter  13

Making Props

Imagination is very helpful for training parrots and also for finding props to use for the tricks you want to teach. Sometimes the idea for the trick comes first; other times it is finding a special prop that inspires an idea for a trick.

Some special props such as bicycles, roller skates, and scooters can cost a lot of money. It is usually because they are difficult to make and must be constructed to fit the size of the bird that is going to use them. Props such as these require materials, tools, imagination, and time. They are typically used by trainers who perform before the public, and so they must be colorful, attractive, and almost indestructible. This usually means they are going to be costly! You can buy such props or have them made for you. If you are imaginative and handy with tools and can find the materials, you can make them. If you aren't rich but are talented and have a few dollars to spend, you can visit hobby and craft shops, novelty stores, toy stores, thrift shops, and garage sales to find potential bird props. (See appendix A, "Resources," for a list of places where you can order props.)

Other sources for props are Internet stores and auction sites. What can you expect to find in these places? Mini skateboards; toy furniture that will fit your parrot; piggy banks; toy telephones; battery-operated toy cars; oversized, standard, and mini playing cards; large and small colored rings; buckets; baskets; flags; ropes; bells; doll baby bottles; doll roller skates; play coins and money; blocks of all sizes and colors; and other colorful items of plastic for teaching colors and the *retrieve*.

For very little money and a lot of imagination you can train your parrot to perform entertaining tricks using inexpensive props.

USING PROPS

Parrots love to pick things up and to move things. They are curious and love to play. For these reasons, they learn tricks using props easily. Props range from simple household objects to electronic toys, and you are limited only by your imagination in your use of them when training your parrot. You might make some of your own simple props and perches, or you might find them available commercially. Some props are objects with other purposes you creatively turn into a prop.

Remember that any prop you choose should be an appropriate size for your bird. It might take some experimentation to come up with a prop that works best for your bird. You many need to try different sizes, materials, or colors before you end up with the perfect prop. Be creative!

One of the cardinal rules of trick training your bird is that props are for performing tricks only. Do not allow your bird to chew on or play with his props. And never, ever leave your pet alone with a prop.

You will find items that can be used as props, and with your creativity you will turn that prop and your parrot's skills into a trick. This is an area where you can use your imagination and have fun with designing your own tricks. That was the case for me when I found a miniature exercise machine at a toy store. It was the perfect size for my bird Cassie to operate. I increased the size of the pedals to accommodate her feet and then taught her to stay on the pedals as they went up and down. It made a cute new trick that I debuted to great success on the TV show *Pet Star*.

GETTING ASSISTANCE

When the task of building and altering props is beyond your skills, look for help from people in other fields of work who have special talents. I found a craftsman who had a shop for making things out of plastic. I told him I wanted a chair for Kiri, my African Grey, to sit in, and I gave him pictures and basic dimensions. I even took Kiri over to his shop so we could see whether the chair would work. The craftsman also took my ideas for a slide, a teeter-totter, and a skateboard and made some excellent props for me. When Squawk, my Blue-crowned Conure, showed she could ride the skateboard really well, he even built a ramp for her out of plastic. Another lucky find was a cabinetmaker who made some of my wooden props, including the "welcome" sign with which Squawk opens my show. Another man who has become a friend turned out to be very innovative. He owns a welding shop. It took him two years, but he did finally make me a bicycle small enough for Squawk. He adapted a flush toilet for Kiri and a jukebox for Squawk. Such people are priceless assets. I encourage you to look for people with similar skills in your community to make any special props you might need.

MAKING YOUR OWN PROPS

For very little money and with a lot of imagination, you can make many of the props for beginning tricks yourself. If you are handy with tools, or have a friend who is, then there are many props you can make. I've described some of them in this chapter. All measurements are taken from my props, which were built for my medium-sized birds: a Blue-crowned Conure, a Caique, and an African Grey. They seem to also work well for smaller birds, but if your bird is larger, change prop dimensions accordingly. All measurements are approximate as it really makes little difference whether a base is 7 or 7½ inches wide or made of heavier material than I have specified. Think twice before making your prop of lighter material, though. Props need to be built sturdily.

T-STAND OR TRAINING PERCH

I'll start with the T-stand, because it is the most important prop you will need to start your training. Luckily there are many available on the Internet and through catalogs, and they seem to come in all sizes so perhaps finding one that way may be the easiest for you. If you want to make your own, here are directions for a

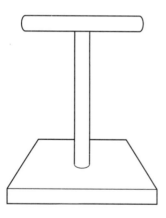

small- to medium-size stand suitable for a small- to medium-size bird.

Use a fairly heavy piece of wood for the base—around 1½ inches thick and cut to 5 by 7 inches. Drill a hole in the center of this block to accommodate an upright dowel 1 inch in diameter by 16 inches tall. Attach a ¾-inch dowel at the top of the pole, to make a crosspiece the bird will use as a perch. The perch should be about 14 inches long. The finished perch will look like a T, thus, the name, T-stand.

FLOOR STAND

Larger birds will probably be more comfortable on a T-stand that sits on the floor. Again, many cage companies sell such stands. I use PVC for the upright on my stand. To make one use a 12 by 12-inch or larger base of wood or other suitably heavy material. To the base attach a PVC holder for a 1½-inch PVC pipe, available at most hardware stores. Cut a length of 1½ inches of pipe about 42 inches long, adjust the length to what works for you, and place it vertically into this holder. Attach a T-shaped PVC holder to the top of this pipe and then use a normal wooden dowel to fit into this top holder. Using a regular wooden dowel instead of PVC is usually easier for your bird to cling to. And there you have a floor perch!

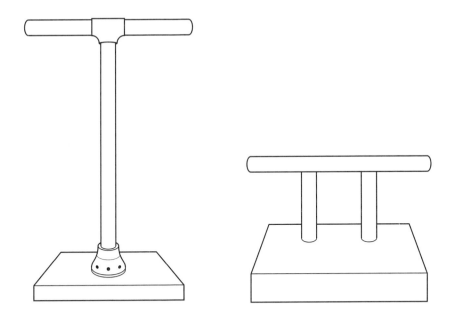

TABLE PERCH

You will use this perch as a place for your bird to go between tricks. It consists of a base, two uprights, and a crosspiece between them, as pictured at above right. The base is 7 by 3 inches and approximately ¾ inch thick. The uprights consist of two pieces of ⅜-inch dowel each 3¼ inches long and supporting a crosspiece 7 inches long made from a ½-inch dowel. Drill two holes in the base approximately 5 inches apart to just fit the uprights. Insert the uprights and glue if you want. Attach the crosspiece, and you have a simple table perch.

RING ON THE PEG

Props for the *ring on the peg* trick are quite simple to make. Cut a ¾-inch-thick piece of board to make a square 4 by 4-inch base. Make the peg of ⁷⁄₁₆-inch doweling about 3 inches long. Drill a hole in the middle of the square base to just fit the peg. Insert the peg so it fits tightly. Glue it in if you want.

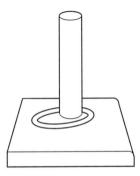

Next get the rings you will use. Get different sizes from ½ inch in diameter up to 2½ inches in diameter. The different size rings should all be the same color for use in teaching size discrimination.

For teaching color discrimination, get three different colored rings, this time all the same size, and in bright colors if possible. Then paint the pegs and bases the same colors as the rings. Now you are ready to teach putting the ring on the peg as well as the related tricks of size and color discrimination.

PUZZLE BOARD

The puzzle board is made of two pieces of wood cut approximately 13½ inches long by 5 inches wide. The board that will become the top board should be about ½ inch thick; the second board will be glued under the top board, and it can be about ¼ inch thick.

Cut three shapes out of the top board to use as your puzzle places. If you cut them out carefully, these pieces can also be used as the "shapes" to fit into these places. Space the three cutout places evenly on the top board. Make sure that your cutout pieces will not fit into any other hole but their correspondingly shaped one. Paint the top board white at this time. Paint each of the cutout shapes a different color. I like to use red, blue, and yellow because they are not only colorful but easy for the

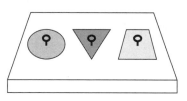

birds to recognize to help them select the correct spot in which to place the shape. Then paint each of the places on the bottom board to match the shape it will hold. Finally, glue the bottom board to the top board so that each shape will show a different color. To finish it off you can paint the bottom and sides of the bottom board white to make a professional-looking prop. Attach screw eyes to the center of each shape to enable your bird to be able to pick each shape up easily.

BASKETBALL HOOP

Teaching a bird to put a ball into a basketball hoop is a popular trick, and there are some commercially available basketball setups. You might want to look at these first to see whether any of them will meet your needs before trying to make one yourself, as the complete setup does require a bit of skill.

If you do want to try to make one yourself, here is one way to proceed. Cut a 5½-inch-square base from a piece of wood approximately ½ inch thick. Select a dowel or pipe about ⅝ inch in diameter and cut to about 8 inches long. Drill a hole in the middle of the base just big enough to accommodate your pole. Make a backboard of a piece of ¼-inch-thick wood, or you could even use a piece of clear plastic. Cut the backboard to approximately 4 by 4 inches and attach it to the dowel.

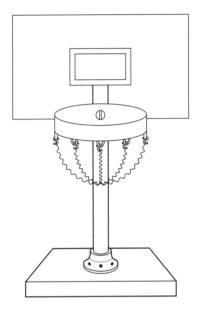

The hoop can be made from a brass ring or a sturdy plastic ring. Attach this ring to the backboard. Attach small lightweight chains to go from one side of the hoop down and across to the other side. Use at least three such chains to form the "basket" for your hoop. Their main purpose is to prevent the ball from dropping on through. It is much more effective for your bird to see the ball remain in the hoop than to have it just drop through.

SHELL GAME

For the very smallest birds, you can use walnut half shells. Try to find three shells that are as close in size and shape as possible. Put a screw eye in the middle of the top of each shell for your bird to use as a handle.

For larger birds I found that the plastic tops from aerosol spray cans work beautifully. Be sure all the tops match, of course. Again, use a screw eye in the center of each top to give the birds something to use for a handle.

For just a little larger "shells" for this game, I found the tops of spray paint cans also were very effective. Of course, you have to buy three cans of identical colored paint to get matching tops, but then, you can always use the paint to spray your props. (Can you visualize all your props painted red?!)

PIGGY BANK

There are loads of piggy banks for purchase out there, and after your bird has learned how to put a coin in a slot one of them might work very well. But to teach the trick, a bank with flat sides and a large slot is most helpful.

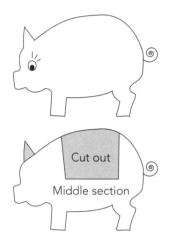

Cut out

Middle section

You can make your own piggy bank with the following template. Enlarge it to fit your particular bird. Cut three identical "piggies" out of ¼-inch-thick wood. Cut a slot out of one of the pieces and also cut off the pig's ears on that piece. Glue this piece between the other two. If you feel the pig tips too easily, you can always make a base and glue the pig to that.

BARBELL/DUMBBELL

Take a short piece of ¼-inch dowel and attach a round fish float, found in sporting goods stores, to each end. Experiment with the length of the dowel and the size of the fish float to fit your particular bird. Paint the whole thing black. For

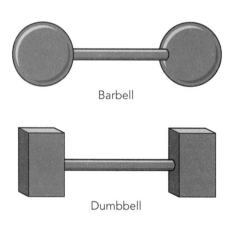

Barbell

Dumbbell

added pizzazz, paint an impressive weight amount, like 50 pounds, in white paint on the float attached to each end.

The dumbbell is similar to the barbell in size, so you can use the same size and length dowel for the center part the bird holds in his beak. Instead of the fish floats, though, substitute a block of wood on each end, again appropriate to the size of your bird. It should look like the dumbbells that dogs use in obedience exercises.

SOCCER FIELD

Start with a flat ½-inch-thick board, about 20 inches long by 11 inches wide. This is your soccer field. Put a trim board around three sides with edges sticking up just high enough to contain the soccer ball. Use two ⅞-inch-diameter dowels cut 8 inches long as uprights and another ¾-inch-diameter dowel to affix between the two uprights as a crosspiece. Drill two holes 7 inches apart near one of the ends of your playing field board to accommodate the two uprights. These become your goal posts. You can paint the soccer field board green if you like to simulate a playing field. Different size mini soccer balls can be found in novelty shops and craft stores. I have even seen them sold on key chains, as well.

HAT RACK

You may be able to buy a hat rack from a source for doll furniture. But to make your own, drill two holes completely through a dowel at different heights, near the top of the pole. Push wire, like clothes hanger wire, through the holes. Bend each end up and trim them off so you end up with four potential hooks to hang a hat on. Attach the pole to a base, and you have a simple hat rack!

You are limited only by your own imagination for further props and for improvising new ways to make the props listed here. Have fun!

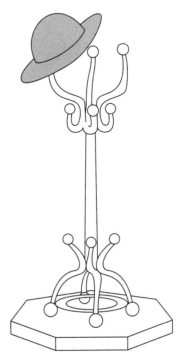

Afterword

Congratulations!

If you have read this book and have taught your parrot some of the tricks I've described, you have come a long way toward understanding your bird and the principles involved in being a trainer. Using the basic *retrieve* command, your bird has learned an array of interesting tricks. When you add tricks from the miscellaneous category, you have a lot of advanced tricks that are fun to do and watch. Don't stop with these tricks. Your imagination is limited only by the bird-size props you can find or make and the creative ways you can ask your bird to retrieve, push, pull, turn, and otherwise manipulate them.

Take advantage of anyone who comes over for a visit to get your parrot to perform. Asking your bird to do tricks in familiar places will make it much easier to get him to show off what he has learned. If you couple that with having your guests exclaim over and praise your bird, you will set the stage for a future performer.

If you have a bird who will talk, but only in front of you and never in front of anyone else, having him do tricks and giving him lots of praise for doing them will make a big difference when you ask your bird to say something. He has seen the attention he gets when he performs; now asking him to say a few words shouldn't be too difficult.

As I have stated, you can train a behavior in many different ways. No one way is perfect for all parrots. I have explained the methods I have used in training my birds, and I know that they work, but if you or your bird do not seem to understand a particular part, be creative; sometimes slightly changing the process makes a big difference.

Each bird is different in the rate at which he learns. If your bird doesn't understand a certain part of a trick at once, this does not necessarily reflect on his intelligence, or yours. His speed of learning largely depends on what he has learned before. The more tricks you teach him, the faster he will learn each succeeding trick. Be patient and set limits with which both you and your parrot can live and be comfortable. The main goal is to have fun and make the experience enjoyable for both of you.

—Tani Robar

Appendix A

Resources

The bird world changes fast, and we're still learning a great deal about our feathered friends. It is wise to keep abreast of the latest information about birds by subscribing to a couple publications and attending a bird seminar at least yearly. Books about many aspects of birds are available and can be treasured resources. When you acquire a bird, a whole world opens to you. The contacts listed here are ways to make that world expand for you and to deepen your understanding of your bird.

To find out more about each resource or whether contact information is outdated on this list, you can do an Internet search. At the time of publication these resources were current, but that could change over time. Be proactive and find out for yourself whether the company or organization is still active or find out whether others are available.

We attempted to include complete information. Some sources do not include all methods of contact; that's because they prefer to be contacted via the media listed. Happy reading!

PERIODICALS

Bird Talk
P.O. Box 6050
Mission Viejo, CA 92690
Phone: (949) 855-8822
Websites: www.animalnetwork.com; www.birdchannel.com

Companion Parrot Quarterly
P.O. Box 819
Loveland, CO 80539
Phone: (970) 278-0233
Website: www.companionparrot.com

Good Bird Magazine
P.O. Box 684394
Austin, TX 78768
Phone: (512) 423-7734
E-mail: Info@goodbirdinc.com
Website: www.goodbirdinc.com

ParrotChronicles.com
P.O. Box 3026
Alameda, CA 94501
E-mail: mailbag@parrotchronicles.com
Website: www.parrotchronicles.com

PARROT PROPS

This is by no means a complete list. For further resources when you are considering purchasing props, search on the Internet, peruse catalogs, and read ads in bird magazines. Internet searches that yield results include bird props, bird trick props, parrot trick training, and parrot training props.

Angel's Playland
2020 Loveland Drive
Florissant, MO 63031
Phone: (314) 831-3345
E-mail: vmgeraci@sbcglobal.net
Website: http://angelbird.bizland.com

Chirp 'n Squawk
323 N. Parkdale Court
Wichita, KS 67203
Phone: (316) 946-0699 or (877) 377-8295
E-mail: BirdSupplies@msn.com
Website: http://birdsupplies.com

Parrot Mountain
1031 Broad Street
Shrewsbury, NJ 07702
Phone: (800) 362-8183
E-mail: sales@parrotmountain.com
Website: https://www.parrotmountain.com/body_startup.asp

Pet Bird Xpress
905 G Street
Hampton, VA 23661
Phone: (757) 245-7675
E-mail: customercare@birdalog.com
Website: www.birdalog.com

BOOKS AND DVDS

Robar Productions (training videos and DVDs)
3767 S. 194th
Seattle, WA 98188
E-mail: tani@parrottricktraining.com
Website: www.parrottricktraining.com

Avian Publications
6380 Monroe Street NE
Minneapolis, MN 55432
Phone: (800) 577-2473
Website: www.avianpublications.com

Read reviews of new books and media releases and talk to others interested in birds and bird training for ideas on further reading for research into bird training. Books to include in an avian reference library include the following:

Athan, Mattie Sue. *Guide to a Well-Behaved Parrot*. Hauppauge, NY: Barron's Educational Series, 1999.

Blanchard, Sally. *Companion Parrot Handbook*. Alameda, CA: Pet Bird Report, 1999.

———. *The Beak Book*. Alameda, CA: PBIC (Pet Bird Information Council) Inc., 2002.

Doane, Bonnie Munro. *My Parrot, My Friend*. Hoboken, NJ: Howell Book House, 1995.

———. *The Pleasure of Their Company*. Hoboken, NJ: Howell Book House, 1998.

Gallerstein, Gary A. *The Complete Bird Owner's Handbook*. Minneapolis, MN: Avian Publications, 2003.

Grindol, Diane, Larry Lachman, and Frank Kocher. *Birds Off The Perch*. New York, NY: Simon & Schuster, 2003.

Grindol, Diane, and Tom Roudybush. *Teaching Your Bird to Talk*. Hoboken, NJ: Howell Book House, 2003.

McCluggage, David, and Pamela Higdon. *Holistic Care For Birds: A Manual of Wellness and Healing*. Hoboken, NJ: Howell Book House, 1998.

Pepperberg, Irene Maxine. *The Alex Studies*. Cambridge, MA: Harvard University Press, 2000.

Speer, Brian L., and Gina Spadafori. *Birds for Dummies*. Hoboken, NJ: Howell Book House, 1999.

TRAINING

Moorpark College
Exotic Animal Training and Management Program
7075 Campus Road
Moorpark, CA 93021
Phone: (805) 378-1400
E-mail: EATM@vcccd.net
Website: www.moorparkcollege.edu/~eatm/index.html

The International Association of Avian Trainers & Educators
350 St. Andrews Fairway
Memphis, TN 38111
Phone: (901) 685-9122
Fax: (901) 685-7233
E-mail: secretary@iaate.org

AVICULTURAL AND VETERINARY GROUPS

American Federation of Aviculture, Inc.
P.O. Box 7312
N. Kansas City, MO 64116
Phone: (816) 421-BIRD
Fax: (816) 421-3214
E-mail: AFAOffice@aol.com
Website: www.afabirds.org

Association of Avian Veterinarians
P.O. Box 811720
Boca Raton, FL 33481-1720
Phone: (561) 393-8901
Fax: (561) 393-8902
E-mail: AAVCTRLOFC@aol.com
Website: www.aav.org

CONTINUING EDUCATION SEMINARS

American Federation of Aviculture, Inc.
P.O. Box 7312
N. Kansas City, MO 64116
Phone: (816) 421-BIRD
Fax: (816) 421-3214
E-mail: AFAOffice@aol.com
Website: www.afabirds.org

Canadian Parrot Symposium
P.O. Box 35065, Hillside Postal Outlet
Victoria, BC, V8T 5G2, Canada
Phone: (250) 477-9982
Fax: (250) 477-9935
E-mail: cparrotsw@shaw.ca
Website: www.parrotsymposium.com/SYM_symposium.htm

The Gabriel Foundation
1025 Acoma Street
Denver, CO 80204
E-mail: gabriel@thegabrielfoundation.org
Website: www.thegabrielfoundation.org

The International Association of Avian Trainers & Educators
350 St. Andrews Fairway
Memphis, TN 38111
Phone: (901) 685-9122
Fax: (901) 685-7233
E-mail: secretary@iaate.org

Mardi Gras Conference
Dr. Greg Rich
3640 West Esplanade
Metairie, LA 70002
Phone: (504) 455-6386
E-mail: DrMardiGra@aol.com
Website: www.gregrichdvm.com

Parrot Education and Adoption Center (PEAC)
P.O. Box 600423
San Diego, CA 92160-0423
Phone: (619) 287-8200
E-mail: parroted@peac.org
Website: www.peac.org

ALTERNATIVE VETERINARY GROUPS

The Academy of Veterinary Homeopathy
P.O. Box 9280
Wilmington, DE 19809
Phone/Fax: (866) 652-1590
Website: www.theavh.org

American Holistic Veterinary Medical Association
2218 Old Emmorton Road
Bel Air, MD 21015
Phone: (410) 569-0795
Fax: (410) 569-2346
E-mail: office@ahvma.org
Website: www.ahvma.org

The American Academy of Veterinary Acupuncture
100 Roscommon Drive, Suite 320
Middletown, CT 06457
Phone: (860) 635-6300
Fax: (860) 635-6400
E-mail: office@aava.org
Website: www.aava.org

CONSERVATION AND RESEARCH GROUPS

Avian Health Network, Inc.
11654 Plaza America Drive #245
Reston, VA 20190
Phone: (703) 481.0676
Website: www.stoppdd.org

The ALEX Foundation
Website: www.alexfoundation.org

Earthwatch Institute
3 Clock Tower Place, Suite 100
P.O. Box 75
Maynard, MA 01754-0075
Website: www.earthwatch.org

RARE Center for Tropical Conservation
1840 Wilson Boulevard, Suite 204
Arlington, VA 22201-3000
Phone: (703) 522-5070
Fax: (703) 522-5027
E-mail: rare@rareconservation.org
Website: www.rareconservation.org

Psittacine Research Project
Dept of Animal Science
University of California
One Shields Avenue
Davis, CA 95616-8521
E-mail: parrots@ucdavis.edu
Fax: (530) 752-0175
Phone: (530) 752-1149
Website: http://animalscience.ucdavis.edu/research/parrot/default.htm

World Parrot Trust—USA
P.O. Box 353
Stillwater, MN 55082
Phone: (651) 275-1877
Fax: (651) 275-1891
E-mail: usa@worldparrottrust.org
Website: www.parrottrustusa.org

ADOPTION AND RESCUE ORGANIZATIONS
The Gabriel Foundation
1025 Acoma Street
Denver, CO 80204
Phone: (303) 629-5900
Fax: (970) 629-5901
E-mail: gabriel@thegabrielfoundation.org
Website: www.thegabrielfoundation.org

Macaw Landing Foundation
P.O. Box 17364
Portland, OR 97217
Phone: (503) 286-0882
E-mail: macaw@macawlanding.org
Website: www.macawlanding.org

Mickaboo Cockatiel Rescue
P.O. Box 1631
Pacifica, CA 94044
E-mail: mail@mickaboo.org
Website: www.mickaboo.org

Mollywood
P.O. Box 28296
Bellingham, WA 98228-0296
Phone: (360) 966-7490
E-mail: mollywood@parrot-rescue.org
Website: www.mollywood.net

National Parrot Rescue & Preservation Foundation (NPRPF)
5116 Bissonnet #471
Bellaire, TX 77401
Phone: (713) 557-BIRD (2473)
Website: www.parrotfestival.org

The Oasis Sanctuary
P.O. Box 30502
Phoenix, AZ 85046
Phone: (520) 212-4737
E-mail: oasis@the-oasis.org
Website: http://the-oasis.org

Parrot Education and Adoption Center (PEAC)
P.O. Box 600423
San Diego, CA 92160-0423
Phone: (619) 287-8200
E-mail: parroted@peac.org
Website: www.peac.org

Appendix B

Places You Can See Performing Birds

This appendix lists some of the places where you can see bird shows featuring performing birds. You can check for more by searching for "Bird Show" or "Parrot Show" on the Internet. You can also check with any theme park you visit to see whether they offer a bird show. Many do! There are also itinerant shows at Renaissance Faires throughout the United States.

Before you travel to see a bird show, check on show and park hours of operation. In states where the winter is harsh, there may be months that shows are not presented, so check first.

Happy trails!

CALIFORNIA

Los Angeles Zoo
5333 Zoo Drive
Los Angeles, CA 90027-1498
Phone: (323) 644-4200
Fax: (323) 662-9786
E-mail: webmaster@lazoo.org
Website: www.lazoo.org

Moorpark College
Exotic Animal and Training Program
7075 Campus Road
Moorpark, CA 93021
Phone: (805) 378-1441
E-mail: EATM@vcccd.net
Website: www.moorparkcollege.edu/~eatm

San Diego Zoo
P.O. Box 120551
San Diego, CA 92112-0551
Phone: (619) 234-3153
Website: www.sandiegozoo.org

San Diego Wild Animal Park
15500 San Pasqual Valley Road
Escondido, CA 92027
Phone: (760) 747-8702
Website: www.sandiegozoo.org/wap/index.html

SeaWorld of California
500 SeaWorld Drive
San Diego, CA 92109
Website: www.seaworld.com/seaworld/ca

Six Flags Marine World
2001 Marine World Parkway
Vallejo, CA 94589
Phone: (707) 643-6722
Website: www.sixflags.com/parks/marineworld/ParkInfo/index.asp

COLORADO

Denver Zoo
2300 Steele Street
Denver, CO 80205-4899
Phone: (303) 376-4800
Fax: (303) 376-4801
E-mail: zooinfo@denverzoo.org
Website: www.denverzoo.org

FLORIDA

Busch Gardens
P.O. Box 9158
Tampa, FL 33674
Phone: (888) 800-5447
Website: www.buschgardens.com/buschgardens/fla

Gulf World Marine Park
15412 Front Beach Road
Panama City Beach, FL 32413
Phone: (850) 234-5271
Website: www.gulfworldmarinepark.com

Parrot Jungle
1111 Parrot Jungle Trail
Miami, FL 33132
Website: www.parrotjungle.com

SeaWorld Orlando
7007 SeaWorld Drive
Orlando, FL 32821
Phone: (800) 327-2424 or (407) 351-3600
Website: www.seaworld.com/seaworld/fla

Zoo World
9008 Front Beach Road
Panama City Beach, FL 32407-4235
Phone: (850) 230-1243

MICHIGAN

Detroit Zoological Park: Belle Isle Zoo
8450 West Ten Mile Road
Royal Oak, MI 48067
Phone: (313) 852-4083
Website: www.detroitzoo.org

MINNESOTA

Minnesota Zoo
13000 Zoo Boulevard
Apple Valley, MN 55124
Phone: (800) 366-7811 or (952) 431-9200
24-hour information line: (952) 431-9500

Fax: (952) 431-9300
E-mail: info@mnzoo.org
Website: www.mnzoo.com

NEVADA

Tropicana Bird Show
3801 Las Vegas Blvd. South
Las Vegas, NV 89119
Phone: (702) 739-2222
Website: www.lasvegaskids.net/las_vegas_attractions/tropicanabirdshow.htm

NEW YORK

The Bronx Zoo
The Wildlife Conservation Society
2300 Southern Boulevard
Bronx, NY 10460
Phone: (718) 220-5100
General information (recording): (718) 367-1010
Website: www.bronxzoo.com

OHIO

Akron Zoo
500 Edgewood Avenue
Akron, OH 44307
Phone: (330) 375-2550
Fax: (330) 375-2575
E-mail: info@akronzoo.org
Website: www.akronzoo.com

Cincinnati Zoo & Botanical Garden
3400 Vine Street
Cincinnati, OH 45220-1399
Phone: (800) 94-HIPPO or (513) 281-4700
E-mail: info@cincinnatizoo.org
Website: www.cincyzoo.org

Columbus Zoo and Aquarium
9990 Riverside Drive
Powell, OH 43065
Phone: (614) 645-3550
Website: www.colszoo.org

Toledo Zoo
2700 Broadway Street
Toledo, OH 43609
Phone: (419) 385-5721
Website: www.toledozoo.org

OKLAHOMA

Oklahoma City Zoo
2101 NE 50th Street
Oklahoma City, OK 73111
Phone: (405) 424-3344
Information: (405) 424-3344
E-mail: info@okczoo.org
Website: www.okczoo.com

Tulsa Zoo
6421 East 36th Street North
Tulsa, OK 74115
Phone: (918) 669-6600
E-mail: tulsazoo@ci.tulsa.ok.us
Website: www.tulsazoo.org

PENNSYLVANIA

National Aviary
Allegheny Commons West
Pittsburgh, PA 15212
Phone: (412) 323-7235
Fax: (412) 321-4364
Website: www.aviary.org

TEXAS

Houston Zoo, Inc.
1513 N. MacGregor
Houston, TX 77030
Phone: (713) 533-6500
E-mail: zooinfo@houstonzoo.org
Website: www.houstonzoo.org

SeaWorld San Antonio
10500 SeaWorld Drive
San Antonio, TX 78251
Phone: (800) 700-7786
Website: www.seaworld.com/seaworld/tx

UTAH

Tracy Aviary
589 East 1300 South
Salt Lake City, UT 84105
Phone: (801) 596-8500
E-mail: info@tracyaviary.org
Website: www.tracyaviary.org

VIRGINIA

Busch Gardens Williamsburg
One Busch Gardens Boulevard
Williamsburg, VA 23187-8785
Phone: (800) 343-7946
Website: www.buschgardens.com/buschgardens/va/default.aspx

WASHINGTON, D.C.

National Zoo
3001 Connecticut Avenue, N.W.
Washington, DC 20008
Phone: (202) 673-4800
E-mail: nationalzoo@nzp.si.edu
Website: http://nationalzoo.si.edu/Visit/default.cfm

RENAISSANCE FAIRES

Bob Bartley
64920 Big Sandy Road
San Miguel, CA 93451
Phone: (805) 239-7060 or (805) 610-4980
E-mail: bob@fowltales.com
Website: www.fowltales.com

Appendix C

Glossary

Aviculturist   One who raises and cares for birds, especially wild birds in captivity.

Behavior   Can be natural or learned, overt or covert. Also, the word *behavior* is used in this book interchangeably with *trick*.

Bridge   A sound, word, light, or any stimulus a bird is trained to recognize that "bridges" the time gap between performance of a behavior and receipt of a reward.

Chaining   Combining separate tricks into a single sequence or performance.

Clicker training   Using a clicker to train your bird. A clicker is a little metal box that makes a clicking sound when pressed. It is used as a bridge (see *bridge*) to tell your bird he has performed whatever action you called for correctly and that a treat/reward will be forthcoming.

Clipping wings   Trimming some or all of a bird's flight feathers (the outermost primary feathers on a bird's wings) to prevent a bird from gaining lift to fly. In pet households, clipping is done for a bird's safety.

Color discrimination   An ability a bird displays to tell the difference among several colors and to choose an appropriately colored object when asked.

Command   Another term for a verbal command.

Construct   Constructs are labels we place on behaviors. They are of limited use because they cannot be measured or universally defined.

Cue   A verbal or a physical signal your bird can hear or see, signaling him to perform a trained behavior.

Fledge In the growth stages of a parrot chick, the stage at which he learns to fly. The age at which a bird fledges varies by species and by individual.

Flighted A bird who has the full capability of flight.

Food deprivation Withholding food before training or a performance.

Generalizing The ability of a parrot to apply what he has learned in one situation to another, different but similar, situation.

Height dominance The theory that a bird may be intractable or more likely to display dominance issues if he is located above your head.

Husbandry skills Behaviors you expect from your bird in everyday living situations, such as entering his cage peacefully, stepping onto your hand or arm, and acceptance of nail and wing trims.

Innovative behaviors Behaviors your bird displays naturally, which do not have to be learned.

Jackpot A reward that is understood by the parrot to be larger or better in quality than the usual reward. Given when a particular behavior has first been perfected, or when a behavior is presented exceptionally well. *To jackpot* is to give a larger than usual reward.

Ladder A prop in the shape of a ladder that a bird can climb easily. *To ladder* is the action of a bird stepping from one finger, hand, or stick to another finger, hand, or stick and then repeating the action.

Luring Enticing a bird to take the next step in learning a trick by offering a treat.

Molding Physically moving your bird into the position you want.

Molt In birds, the cyclical shedding and replacing of feathers.

Operant conditioning The process that happens whenever any creature performs a behavior and then learns from the consequences of its actions.

Performing In trick training parlance, this usually means showing the tricks your bird has learned to other people. This may be a friend or a relative or could be an audience viewing a series of tricks that are chained together and narrated, comprising a show.

Positive reinforcement A training method in which you immediately reward any behavior you are trying to shape (teach) and ignore any wrong moves or behaviors. The bird must have some reason to repeat a behavior, and the reward is the reason.

Positive reward method   Tani Robar's method of teaching tricks. Praise and rewards (see *P&R*) are given with each approximation until the final behavior is obtained, which is then jackpotted.

P&R   Praise and reward. The reward can be anything deemed desirable by the bird: food, scratches, petting, attention, and so on. Food is recommended as the most reliable reward.

Presentation   The pleasing visual aspect of a show for an audience. When you train your bird to take objects to the front of the training table toward the audience instead of to you, you are thinking about how a show will look for an audience.

Prop   A shortened version of the theatrical term *property,* used in this book to describe any object handled or used by either the handler or the bird in the performance of a trick.

Recall   Teaching your bird to come to you upon a verbal or a physical cue.

Retrieve   A behavior concept you can teach your bird that is the basis for many tricks. In the *retrieve,* your bird picks up any object you designate and brings it to you or places it where you direct.

Reward   Usually a food treat given to a bird after he has performed a desired behavior on cue. A reward could also be verbal praise, a head scratch, or some rough and tumble play, if that is what your bird likes. A reward is something that communicates "job well done."

Scritch   A term commonly used by companion parrot owners meaning to scratch a parrot's head, usually against the grain of the feathers; a form of petting a parrot.

Shaping   Developing a behavior by accepting a small step toward the behavior at first and gradually demanding performance closer to the full behavior.

Show   A series of trained tricks narrated with a story line and performed for an audience. A show is often humorous and may involve performances by more than one bird.

Socialized   In this book we mean a bird who is comfortable being handled, being restrained, turned over, and cuddled and who will accept food from your fingers. This is the first stage of trick training and is important in later stages when you will handle your bird to show him how to perform a trick.

T-stand   A stand with a single support and a top bar (so it looks like a capital letter T). A T-stand is used for training and for anytime you need a designated perching place for your bird. T-stands can either be floor models or can be smaller and sit on a table.

Table perch   A place for a small bird to sit on the training table between tricks. Often a short perch with a support at each end, mounted to a base.

Targeting   A shaping procedure in which your bird is trained to follow a target stick and touch it when asked. A target stick can be anything you choose, even your fist will work. Possible target stick choices could be a chopstick, a knitting needle, a wooden dowel, or a wooden spoon.

Toweling   Method used to capture and restrain a companion parrot. It is less stressful for a bird if he has learned to accept being toweled.

Trainer   A person working with a bird to teach him behaviors and commands.

Training area   A relatively quiet area, free from distractions and out of sight of the bird's own cage, in which to train.

Training session   Time spent training a bird. Number and length of sessions depends on your schedule and your bird's response to training.

Training table   A table located in a quiet area of your home, on which you practice tricks. It is advantageous for the training table to have a lip or raised edge around it so that balls won't roll off or your bird won't sail off the edge when you are training a rolling prop behavior such as skates, scooter, bicycle, or skateboard.

Treat   Any food item deemed especially desirable by your bird. Usually awarded to your bird for performing a trained behavior.

Treat getter   An object a bird associates with getting a treat.

Trick   Used interchangeably in this book with the term *behavior*. Refers to a trained behavior that is performed on cue.

Trick training   The discipline of teaching a bird to perform on cue using positive rewards only and no punishment or harsh methods.

Verbal command   An auditory cue that tells your bird what behavior to perform.

Visual cue   A hand gesture that tells your bird what trick to perform.

Weaned   A young bird who no longer needs to be hand-fed or fed by his parents. The bird has all of his feathers and can eat and drink on his own. This varies by species, but for most parrots, this period happens between the ages of 6 weeks and 6 months. Prior to weaning, a parrot chick is dependent on his bird parents or human caretakers for feeding, warmth, and some grooming.

Wing trimming   Clipping the primary flight feathers on both wings of a parrot for safety and training purposes. This must be done after every molt as the feathers grow back in. Not to be confused with pinioning, a permanent way to impede the flight of waterfowl.

Index

About the Authors

Tani Robar is a professional animal trainer who has spent years training performing animals and teaching others to train their animals. She has been acclaimed for her ability to develop and perfect unique training methods that allow her students to teach their pets an almost unlimited variety of skills and behaviors. For the last fifteen years Tani has been putting on bird shows, giving lectures, and helping others to teach their birds to do tricks. Besides appearing on TV and writing articles on bird training, she has produced four videos/DVDs to help people visualize how to teach their parrots a variety of skills and tricks. These videos are sold internationally. She recently appeared three times on Animal Planet's *Pet Star* TV show and won the top place on one of the segments with Cassie, her Black-headed Caique.

Tani's outstanding results are obtained by knowledge and skill, never by cruel methods. The adoration her birds so obviously show is further proof of the worth of this kind of training. Her performing birds are also her companions and share her life, including sharing meals with her and her family.

Growing up with many animals, Tani found that the most interesting part of owning animals was training them. The first pets she can remember were bantam chickens, which she carried around with her, taught to come when called, and trained to pick at spiders discovered in the house. Soon the neighborhood dogs were coming when she called and were performing simple tricks she taught them. Finally she got her own dog, a pint-size, wire-haired fox terrier, and they became inseparable companions. She started honing her skills, and soon the dog was performing an amazing number of tricks. She won her first contest at age seven showing all the tricks her dog could do at a pet competition. She never looked back. She has trained enumerable animals since then and won many prizes.

Professionally, Tani started out training horses and later teaching dog obedience classes and showing in the obedience ring. Her own dog, a collie, was only the third dog in the state of Washington to receive its Utility degree. She first started teaching obedience classes for the Washington State Obedience Training Club and then for the YMCA. Then she taught guard dog training for Western Metro Guard Dog Association. But it wasn't until her last German Shepherd had to be put to sleep from a degenerative nerve problem that she turned her attention to training birds. Still devastated from losing her last great companion dog, she looked at the bird she then owned, a normal grey Cockatiel, and thought, "Well, if I can train big dogs, I can certainly train a little bird." And so began her present preoccupation with parrots.

Tani attended Stanford University. She then went on to obtain a degree in psychology from the University of Washington. Tani has been a research associate in the field of child development and human relations for the past forty years. (She's a homemaker and the mother of two adult sons.) Tani resides in Seattle.

Diane Grindol grew up in Rolling Meadows, Illinois. She met a male cockatiel named Clement when she moved to Monterey, California, in 1982 and within a couple weeks acquired her own normal gray hen, which turned out to be a life-altering event. Dacey lived for twenty-two years and added her wisdom to many projects. Diane wrote a pet column for the American Cockatiel Society for six years and produced a set of videos about Cockatiel care and breeding in 1988. She founded the Monterey Bay Cage Bird Club and was its program coordinator for ten years. She edited and published a companion bird journal, *Bird World*, for two years.

Diane traveled to Guatemala in 1993 with a UC Davis field biologist to observe parrots in the wild, an inspiring and treasured experience in her bird life. Since 1996 Diane has coordinated companion bird seminars in California, Seattle, and Chicago. She frequently speaks to bird clubs and at national conventions or seminars.

Since 1995 Diane has written a column for *Bird Talk Magazine*. She currently is the Web editor of BirdChannel.com for BowTie, Inc. Her other books include *The Complete Book of Cockatiels, Cockatiels For Dummies, Birds Off The Perch,* and *Teaching Your Bird to Talk.* Diane lives on the Monterey Peninsula, California, and shares her life with a small flock of Cockatiels, a Blue-headed Pionus parrot, and a guinea pig.